Ismail Merchant's

INDIAN
CUISINE

Ismail Merchant's
INDIAN
CUISINE

A
Joan
Kahn
BOOK

ST. MARTIN'S PRESS / NEW YORK

Photographs courtesy of Meryl Joseph.

ISMAIL MERCHANT'S INDIAN CUISINE. Copyright © 1986 by Ismail Merchant.
Photos copyright © 1986 by Meryl Joseph. All rights reserved. Printed in the United
States of America. No part of this book may be used or reproduced in any manner
whatsoever without written permission except in the case of brief quotations embod-
ied in critical articles or reviews. For information, address St. Martin's Press, 175
Fifth Avenue, New York, N.Y. 10010.

Design by Giorgetta Bell McRee

Copy editor: Joan Whitman

"A Joan Kahn Book"

Library of Congress Cataloging-in-Publication Data

Merchant, Ismail.
    Ismail Merchant's Indian cuisine.

    1. Cookery, India.   I. Title.   II. Title:
Indian cuisine.
TX724.5.I4M47   1986   641.5954   86-13825
ISBN 0-312-43752-8

First published in Great Britain by Macdonald/Futura.
First U.S. Edition
10 9 8 7 6 5 4 3 2 1

Contents

Acknowledgments

*I*t is a simple thing to tell one's friends, "I am writing a cookbook," but doing so has turned out to be a very painstaking and meticulous operation, even something of a chore, which for me actual cooking never is. So in trying to put this all together I often became very impatient. My approach to cooking has always been pragmatic and experimental (not so different really from the way I go about finding the finance for my films).

This book wouldn't have been possible without the help of my colleague and friend, Dick Robbins, who composed the music for several of our recent films, from *The Europeans* to *A Room with a View*. He has gone through every recipe, testing ones he wasn't familiar with, and then arranging them, ingredient by ingredient, instruction by instruction, for the whole book. I don't think I could have got through without his attention to tiny details, something essential for any successful recipe.

Going back further, I must thank Jim Ivory not only for his encouragement in this present venture, but for his patience when, after a hard day, it was easier to make qeema (minced meat) than adrak aur shazeera-walli ran (roast lamb), or to warm up some dal, rather than to shop for all the tasty treats he so looks forward to.

I would like to thank Scott Ewing, a freelance editor I met through my publisher, who rechecked all the recipes, testing many of them, and prepared the final text of the recipes for the printers. I am also grateful to Begum Sabeeha Ahmed Husain for helping me with suggestions of Indian names for the recipes.

Finally, my thanks to Ruth Prawer Jhabvala, who has eaten my food with enthusiasm and encouraged me by her amazed comments on the speed with which I conjure up a meal.

Ismail Merchant's
INDIAN CUISINE

1
Introduction

My friends say that my cooking is different from anything they have known. They call me a master chef and encourage me repeatedly to write a cookery book, a difficult undertaking as most of my time is spent making films. At last I relent and herein present some of my recipes, ideas on cooking, and several stories about and from friends who have enjoyed my cooking—a section of stories from my friends follows this introduction.

So what makes a master chef? For me it means that he or she must have imagination, a flair for mixing conventional and unconventional ingredients, an appreciation of different seasonings, and a desire for praise to satisfy his or her ego. A great cook should be able to do something well with the snap of a finger rather than to toil over it. He or she should be inventive, be someone who can whip up something from nothing. From two pieces of straw a master should be able to make a grand salad—well almost.

Now, you may not ever want to be a master chef, but anyone can learn certain techniques and basic methods which will produce delicious dishes. I have taught quite a few of my friends to do so. And some of you may even have a great talent waiting to be awakened. If this book inspires you, that's splendid; I want to help you please others by showing you how to cook delicious dishes for them, quickly and with as much ease as possible. My greatest challenge is to encourage you through my recipes to be adventurous and not be afraid to make discoveries. The tightrope act of whipping up a meal for several important guests in half an hour can be saved for later!

My own knowledge of food and cooking developed gradually. I was born into a middle-class family in Bombay, with six sisters, all of whom are superb cooks. My father never cooked, but he appreciates good food. Men were generally not allowed in the kitchen, so male family members never had an opportunity actually to cook. In India when I was growing up most middle-class families had a cook as well as someone to do the shopping. My mother supervised everything, though she too was and still is a first-rate cook. I could freely invite twenty guests home and everything would be provided for, the most perfect menu with eight or ten dishes. But I could only appreciate the meal, never be directly involved.

Before leaving India I became familiar with Chinese cooking, but in America I learned about French, Italian, and many other fine culinary traditions. I would often go to a small French restaurant that I could afford on Ninth Avenue and 55th Street in Manhattan, The Brittany, have dinner, and talk to the people there about food. Later, I spent a lot of time in France. Consequently, my cooking is not always purely Indian. Sometimes it is a combination of French and Indian. There are definitely some lighter elements in it from nouvelle cuisine. By the same token, when I make a spaghetti sauce, it's Italo-Indian. As with every chef, my cooking is the result of many influences, but it remains essentially Indian.

It was in America that I actually learned to cook. As an Indian host I could not offer my guests hamburgers and hot dogs. They expected something more exotic. Saeed and Madhur Jaffrey were among the first to taste my cooking. Madhur wasn't cooking much then and in a way she and I were in the same boat. We wanted to recreate in New York

City the Indian flavors we had grown up with. I remember one of the first meals I prepared for them when Saeed brought Madhur from the hospital with their firstborn, Zia. I prepared it in their tiny apartment on West 27th Street with O. Henry's ghost hovering around the kitchen. Saeed had warned me that occasionally the ghost appeared and I was convinced that my cooking disturbed his simple palate.

So in 1958, wanting to please my American friends, I learned how to do all the things I was not allowed to do in India: the cooking, all the shopping, and the serving. In the United States one has to do everything and it is best if you enjoy it; fortunately I do. I discovered that my cooking developed into more than just a way to please my friends. It helped me make headway in my profession. I have invited writers, actors, financiers, bankers, and all sorts of interesting—and useful—people involved in all aspects of filmmaking home for dinner. I like to think that my cooking and the occasion softened some of them up a bit.

A successful evening is one in which your guests experience something unique. Naturally you want a spectacular success, with guests heaping you with compliments before they wander off happily into the night. I maintain that this is possible without days, or even a day, of preparation. Part of a good cook's success, as I have said, has to do with speed.

One summer evening after a concert I invited some guests (of the useful sort) home for a late supper. I first served them wine—never mixed drinks, which would confuse their palates and other senses. I also served some poppadums; then excused myself because I wanted to start cooking. They became quite panicky, glancing nervously at watches and suggesting it might, after all, be best to go to a restaurant. I insisted, "Enjoy a glass of wine, and in half an hour everything will be ready." They didn't seem very reassured. Earlier, however, I had bought striped bass, broccoli, and salad ingredients and already had plenty of rice. Within half an hour I appeared from the kitchen with the four dishes. My guests could not believe that all this could be prepared so quickly, including refilling their glasses, darting in for some quick conversation, darting out for some essential phone calls, organizing background music, more poppadums, and so on. It was, they all told me, a memorable evening.

For years I never dared mention to my mother and sisters that I had learned to cook. I never told them that I could make something very nice in half an hour. But when I was visiting Bombay a few years ago, one day my mother wasn't feeling well. My sister Rukhsana had brought some huge prawns home and I told her I wanted to do something with them "in the French style." Telling everybody to relax in the sitting room, I shut myself in the kitchen. I cooked the prawns in a mustard sauce, which isn't actually so foreign for Indians; Bengalis cook seafood and fish in a mustard sauce every day. I noticed my sister looking through a crack in the kitchen door and overheard her telling the others that I was going to make a mess or burn myself, but in less than fifteen minutes, I brought the huge prawns out, serving them as an hors d'oeuvre.

Everyone was surprised and pleased, if somewhat alarmed, at my revelation of this new talent, for in orthodox Indian households the men of the family definitely stay out of the kitchen. My sister Rukhsana did say the prawns were not prepared as well as she would have done; they were not pure Indian, but in an "adulterated" style. However, she confessed that she loved eating them. After a little while she asked me, "What did you put in it?" Since then I have cooked many times for my family, though it is still hard for the women to get used to the idea that I can cook something delicious so quickly. It still seems a little beyond their imagination, but now, whenever I want to use their kitchen, they go into the sitting room and pretend to relax.

As a child my time in the kitchen was spent urging whoever was cooking to hurry up with their preparations. I had no idea then that cooking would later interest me so much. I was simply hungry and wanted to eat. When I came home from school for the noontime break, I could smell the wonderful aromas coming from the kitchen as I ran up the stairs. As we had only one hour to go home, eat lunch, and return to school, I would immediately begin agitating in the kitchen, growling and stomping about. The cooks would say they were trying to hurry, but they never changed their pattern of cooking, no matter how much I urged. Everything took a certain amount of time, and I had to wait. If I wanted to go back to school hungry, I was welcome to do that.

For lunch there would usually be fish, rice, bread, vegetables, and dal. Pomfret was the favorite fish, often cooked with a coconut sauce. I preferred fish because it doesn't take as long as meat or chicken. These latter took longer to cook and, in my schoolboy opinion, were best served at night. Weekends were different; then the major meal was at midday.

When I return to Bombay, I always visit the market where I shopped as a child with my father. I go to look for fresh seasonal vegetables and fruit and to enjoy the spectacle and aroma of fresh produce—fish, meat, and spices. Though it is one of the most pleasurable things to do in the city, it is a pity that few foreigners ever visit the huge Crawford Market in Bombay, an area modeled on London's Covent Garden. Now Covent Garden is a center of designer boutiques and smart restaurants, where the only vegetables you'll see are in ragouts, but the great stone and cast-iron structure that houses Crawford Market is still a very active place of commerce. Its vendors sit in a beautiful light filtered down from high skylights, making their vegetables and fruits look like jewels. The vendors preside over their stalls like so many Aladdins, a funny mixture of an oriental bazaar and nineteenth-century England.

In London today, if you shop in Berwick Street in Soho or another open market with its pyramids of cabbages and so forth, you get something of the flavor of shopping in the bazaar in Bombay. But any market which has an attractive display of fresh vegetables and fruit is superior to the general supermarket. I'm sure part of the success of the Korean fruit and vegetable stands in Manhattan is the visual impression of heaped-up yet artfully arranged goods not unlike the displays found in good florists (and not unlike in price, either).

Now some words on kitchens and equipment. My own tiny

kitchen must be one of New York's smallest. If readers were to see it, they might disbelieve my claims of having effortlessly tossed off the little dinner parties for which I have become well known. The kitchen measures 5½ by 8 feet and has no other equipment than a four-ring gas stove and an oven. My little dinner parties *do* cost something in effort, and timing is all important, but restricted kitchen space is almost an Indian tradition. Most Indian cooks prepare superb meals of many dishes crouched over a spirit-burner set on the floor. There are no modern microwave ovens in Indian kitchens, not even in a rich man's house. A cook usually makes do with a two-burner gas stove, shifting the pots backward and forward as need arises. It's a bit like that in New York. The kitchens in the house in upstate New York and in my flat in London are different affairs, but like millions of other New Yorkers, I have to make do in a sort of broom closet, and have been doing so for twenty years.

Once I imported a proper English gas cooker into India so my mother and sisters would not have to squat on the floor in traditional fashion. They could stand to cook or even sit in front of it, but the cooker stood unused in a corner, covered with a khaki cloth until it was finally sold to neighbors. I don't think they ever used it much either.

Except for a food processor, I have very basic cooking utensils. The food processor has helped me to create certain dishes and to do some traditional chores with great ease and speed. Though it's a very good kitchen tool, and fun too, it is not a necessity. Whenever I mention combining ingredients in a food processor or blender, I know that the ingredients can be combined by hand instead. It simply takes longer. My other cooking utensils include three or four saucepans of various sizes; a few frying pans, all with covers; sharp knives; a grater for ginger; and a chopping board.

It's the ingredients, not the equipment, that should be special, and the way you combine them. My own larder includes bay leaves, Dijon and coarse-grained mustards, good tarragon vinegar, vegetable oil for cooking and good olive oil for salads, and a ready collection of dried spices from which I make up my masala—or seasoning—mixtures. Sometimes these mixtures include items such as green chiles, parsley, coconut, and coriander, which I buy fresh for the occasion. Whether or not my masalas contain fresh ingredients, I always mix them on the spot before I start cooking. Apart from marinades, I think that too much advance preparation spoils the flavors of spice mixtures. There follows a list of what I consider the most important spices to have on hand. Other spices and ingredients I use in this book are available in most Indian shops if not in your local supermarket.

Black pepper *(kali mirch)* should be bought whole as peppercorns and freshly ground. I use it liberally in almost all of my cooking.

Caraway seeds *(shazeera)* are gathered from a plant native to both Asia and Europe. This spice is used mostly in north Indian cooking. It's best to grind the seeds a little in a pestle and mortar just before using them to bring out their flavor.

Cardamom *(elaichi)* comes in two basic types, the smaller pale green or white pods and the larger black or "wild" pods. Sometimes the tiny black seeds are removed from the pods and crushed to use in cooking, but I usually use the whole pods in my recipes; it's easier. People just leave them on the side of their plate.

Cayenne pepper *(lal mirch)*, also called "red powder" in Indian grocers, is basic to Indian cooking. I've used modest amounts of it in my recipes, so you may prefer to add more once you taste the dish.

Garlic *(lasson)*. During the cold season my mother always made a bread with fresh green garlic as it provides warmth and comfort. In the West garlic is not so indulged in as it has a very strong aroma. People tend to avoid you when you have eaten a garlicky meal, so it is not a time to try and get close to somebody. In India the effect is the opposite. I love garlic in my food and particularly use it with lentil dishes, for which I make baghar, frying chopped garlic in oil until it browns. Add it as a garnish.

Ginger *(adrak)* is a knobbly growth on the root, not the root itself. Sometimes I don't bother, but its thin skin should really be peeled before grating or chopping, especially if using it in a purée. Rarely if ever do I use dried ground ginger.

Mustard seeds *(sarson)*. Both yellow and black mustard seeds are used in Indian cooking. I prefer the black ones because of the way they look in a dish, but yellow ones do nicely. The seeds are also made into a fairly spicy oil and, of course, into prepared mustards.

Saffron *(zaffran)* is sold dried both as yellow-red threads and powdered—expensive in either form, but only a little of this very important spice is needed. Many sweets, rice pilafs, and chicken dishes would pine for lack of it.

Salt *(namak)* is used in amounts according to personal preference. I can't bear to cook without it.

Turmeric *(haldi)* is sold ground and gives a mild flavor and yellow color to dishes in which it is used—as well as bright yellow stains to skin and cloth, so be careful.

Chiles, red and green *(lal mirch* and *hari mirch)* vary in heat and spiciness, the red ones being dried and the fresh ones green. When I find a good variety of whole dried chiles, about two inches long, I buy a supply and keep them on hand in a jar. Fresh green ones are always to be found in the vegetable drawer of my refrigerator. They vary in size from two to four inches, and contain many white seeds, some or all of which you can leave in, if you like spicier food.

Cinnamon *(dar cheeni)* comes from the paper-thin bark of a tree, rolled inside one another into sticks. These have so much more flavor than ground cinnamon that I use the sticks whole or broken whenever I want the flavor of cinnamon in my dishes.

Cloves *(lavang)* should be used whole for their superior flavor and splendid fragrance.

Coriander *(dhania)* is one of my very favorite spices. Fresh coriander is now sold at many greengrocers. The wonderful flavor and aroma of the fresh green leaves are added toward the end of cooking in many dishes. More familiar is ground coriander, though in my opinion it is better to grind the coriander seeds yourself, or best of all use fresh coriander leaves.

Cumin *(zeera)* is used whole and ground. As with coriander seeds, for flavor and fragrance it is best to grind whole cumin seeds into powder just before you use them. I use an electric coffee mill for this purpose and keep another one for grinding coffee.

A Note on Titles

There are a number of dishes in the book for which the Indian names appear very westernized. This is because there are no equivalent names for these in Hindi or Urdu. Some of the words, like "cutlets," "patties," "omelets," and "chops" are used in daily cooking, but their spelling and pronunciation are completely Indianized. "Cutlet" would be written and pronounced as *cutless*, omelet as *aam-late*, patties as *paytees*, and mutton chop as *mutton chap*. Even in a small-town restaurant in India the menu refers to *aam-late, paytees,* and *cutless*. Of course the recipes are more exotic and the use of spices is heavy, but the words themselves have been borrowed from English in the long association with the British in India.

2

Some Friends Comment . . .

Fast Family Food

One—hopefully—chooses to remember the parental table in loving detail, recalling long-gone meals, particular dishes that seem never to taste as good anywhere else. "Mother had some secret ingredient," one says, or perhaps it was Father, if he lent a hand. One goes out into the world with these memories and in time Mother and Father disappear and someone else takes over cooking for you, or you learn to do it for yourself and, if you do not lead too rootless an existence, the old memories out of the kitchens of childhood are overlaid with new ones. This has happened to me, and now my family table is presided over by Ismail, so that as I approach my second childhood it is the tastes and aromas of *his* food that overwhelmingly colors my memories of eating at home. When I do not get his cooking for a while due to separation or to being on the road with some film, I crave it. It has now become a part of me, if not in the actual physical sense (though it could well be that, too), then certainly overwhelmingly in my perception of what is good in life.

When I first knew Ismail in New York in 1961, had in fact just met him, it was decided to throw a little party in my walk-up apartment on East 62nd Street and to invite the friends we knew mutually, most of whom were Indian, for dinner, where I would screen a (very) rough cut of the documentary I was working on that later became *The Delhi Way*. And it was the usual somewhat alarming situation, with guests arriving and no activity in the kitchen, not even a brown paper bag or two from Gristedes, expensively and reassuringly lopsided and crammed-looking. What there was was a mess of pakoras and samosas, quite cold, quite greasy, that had been brought in from a somewhat forlorn Indian restaurant—one of two in the city then—in the Times Square area called The Kashmir, which was the regular haunt of Saeed Jaffrey in those days. He had also been invited to our party. I say "our," but who do I mean? It was supposed to be *my* party, and I have never had to give one since, because Ismail just takes over, grand Indian host that he is. Chilled wine bottles appear out of the sky, qeema, dal, and rice are suddenly in evidence (or even better things) as the catered hors d'oeuvres from the Kashmir restaurant are giving out, and everyone is happy. So it was that night, so it is every night whether there are guests or not, if we happen to be in the same country: the fast family food, some of it rough and ready, some of it leftover, some of it of a surpassing freshness and delicacy of ingredient and inspiration. This is what I know, this is what I remember.

—*James Ivory*

Working on Recipes

Ever since we met, whenever the opportunity arose, I've hung about Ismail's kitchen, a gourmet-chef groupie. Groupies can be supportive and, I hope, good company at times, but we can also be troublesome. For example, we like to ask questions about what's going on. Not that Ismail doesn't like sharing his knowledge, on the contrary, he loves it. It's just that he cooks very quickly and there is little time for both concentrating on cooking and explaining what he is doing.

Questions can interrupt his flow, but occasionally I have broken through. "What was that?"

"What?"

"What you just put in?"

"That was black cardamom."

"How many?"

"Well, that was . . . seven . . . pods."

Being an inspirational cook, Ismail is not one to quibble over small amounts of ingredients when he's making a favorite dish. Peering over his shoulder, many have been impressed with his speed, his confidence, his command of his tools, his knowledge of ingredients and, most importantly for me, his fun in cooking. He has great joy in preparing something wonderful, especially when he serves it to others. He loves to please people and has a great time doing it.

Ismail has taught me to cook and I feel I can manage now quite well. I believe that anyone can by following his recipes, approaching them with the same spirit in which they were created. They will also discover the pleasure and satisfaction that comes from making something delicious for someone else.

Once, feeling very bold, I asked, "Ismail, can you remember ever making a mistake in the kitchen?" With a look of bewilderment he answered, "Of course not."

Could this really be so, I thought? And I considered the

number of pots with rice burnt on the bottom that I have scrubbed clean. But to Ismail, burning rice is not a "mistake"; it is not important at all. It's rather like dropping a spoon; such things happen sometimes. The only real mistake would be in not trying to please one's guests, and he has never failed to try to please them. He tries with all his heart, because he enjoys it so, and because he enjoys it so, he tries with all his heart.

—*Richard Robbins*

Dining with Ismail

Dining with Ismail is always an adventure. If you dine at his home you know you will be well fed. If he invites you to dine out, the chances are that he has accepted an invitation to dinner and is taking you along as an unexpected guest. So, if you give a dinner party and invite Ismail, you had better prepare for the odd extra guest or two. Better still, ask Ismail to cook for you. I always do.

When I moved back to London in the early 70s, my fourth-floor walk-up flat at 82 Cornwall Gardens became Ismail's home in London. As I had just moved in I had no furniture except beds, a couple of carpets, and an ancient octagonal dining table I had bought with five uncomfortable rickety chairs from the owners of "Beechwood," the house outside New York City where we filmed *Savages*. In my living room I placed four unmatched upright chairs in front of a monster TV set which I had got so that we and twenty friends could watch the first broadcast of our film, *Autobiography of a Princess,* at home. This strange collection of uncomfortable furniture did not deter Ismail from having people over for meals.

One morning Ismail announced that he had invited Ingrid Bergman to tea the next day and that the four chairs in the living room would not do. I was delighted at the prospect of meeting Miss Bergman, so I went straight out and hurriedly bought a rather odd-looking pair of sofas, to be delivered immediately—but it wasn't soon enough. Ismail, not knowing of my purchase and thinking that Miss Bergman deserved better than the four flights of steep stairs and the discomfort of my flat, had changed his mind and invited her to take tea with him at Claridges instead. And that, to my regret, was how Miss Bergman never sat on my new sofas.

But many friends did make it up all those stairs and were rewarded by heavenly smells of exotic foods and delicious meals. Although it is difficult to pick one evening from the many when unusual and adventurous meals—for English palates—were proudly produced, there was an occasion I do remember as being remarkable. This time, in addition to Jim Ivory, Ismail, and me, there was Ruth Jhabvala, a visiting film mogul, and his wife. As Ismail handed round unusually strong drinks, he quietly asked me, "Where's the fish?"

"What fish?" I countered.

"Didn't you get the fish and the broccoli and . . . ?"

"No, I thought you said you would," I stammered.

"Do we have any food at all?" Ismail's voice was getting louder.

"Absolutely nothing," I whispered in a panic. "I'll dash out!"

"First let's look in the refrigerator," said Ismail, comparatively calm.

We went to look: a few eggs, five sprigs of tired parsley, half a carton of yoghurt, some cooked rice, two wrinkled lemons, last night's cold string beans, and in the freezer, half a package of pita bread. All in all, it was a small assortment of odds and ends. Ismail looked serious. "I'll see what I can do," he said, like a surgeon facing a particularly difficult operation. Only too willingly I left him to it.

Fourteen minutes later, Ismail blithely emerged from the kitchen bearing a tray laden with a spectacular egg curry with rice, raita, dal, potatoes, onions, string beans in lemon butter, hot pita bread, and his mother's famous green mango chutney from Bombay. A feast fit for a mogul. If I had not witnessed this miracle of speed and culinary alchemy I would have assumed that Ismail had been planning the menu for days. I think that even Ingrid Bergman would happily have put up with the steep stairs and a hard chair for this meal.

—Anthony Korner

The Producer as Foodie

To know Ismail is to eat with him—or, more likely, to be fed by him. He knows that the way to an actor's art is through his stomach, and he shamelessly deploys this knowledge to obtain your services, your quiescence, your goodwill. The phrase "to curry favor" was probably invented with Ismail in mind.

And what curries! We had already known each other for some years before I supped at his table. This was a mere oversight on Ismail's part, or, rather, a lapse of memory which I was too shy to correct.

"You remember that wonderful dinner I gave in Paris that you gatecrashed with Peggy Ramsay?" I didn't, for several good reasons. Peggy and I had not been in Paris at the same time, I had just slipped fleetingly onto the set of *Quartet,* and would rather have died than gatecrash a group of people who knew each other but not me. "Yes," I nonetheless lied, because it seemed so much easier, and somehow less disappointing, "yes, what a marvelous meal that was!" So whenever Ismail and I bumped into each other, he would jovially recall the now legendary meal, and the memory of it would grow rosier and rosier.

One evening we went to see a play of shattering ponderousness, and as we joyously fled at the interval, Ismail (to whom an evening without a meal would be an offence against nature) steered us swiftly towards the excellent Vietnamese restaurant in Firth Street. As we awaited our dishes, he started to regale our fellow diners with the mythic meal, and with my breathtaking audacity in the gatecrashing department. Suddenly he broke all the rules and asked me, "What was it we had that evening? I don't remember."

"Well," I paused, "uh, curry?"

"Yes, yes, of course there was curry, but what *kind* of curry?" My experience of Indian food was at that time limited to fairly bitter memories of late-night poppadums in provincial towns, so I gawped somewhat.

"Er, wasn't it, er, snail curry, I thought, with capers, and um, chestnuts," thinking, France and he probably used all the local stuff.

A smile of apparent recollection spread over his face. "Of course," he said, "what a wonderful memory you have, even for ingredients. Wonderful!"

Since then I have had many marvelous curries with Ismail, none better than those on the set of *A Room with a View* in Florence. It is, however, agonizing to watch the poor man torn between being a host and being a producer. He is passionately eager that you should consume his magical concoctions, as much and as late as you like, and equally passionate that you should appear on the set next morning fresh, on time, and not too fat.

"Eat!" he cries, "but quickly! And not too much! But have you had any of this? You must, I insist! I've called you a cab, you can have another helping of dal while you wait. Take it with you! Yes, yes, but *go,* I implore you."

—*Simon Callow*

Friend's Observation

England breeds an organized and generally rather prescribed way of living. I escaped from this when I lived for two years in Italy, where spontaneity and last-minute feasts are the order of the day. However, that was sixteen years ago, and when Ismail and I plotted a jointly hosted, Merchant cuisine evening at my flat in the Albany, I set about the preparations with the customary advanced planning. Six guests were invited by Ismail and five by me. It was to be a gourmet evening and an occasion when Marion Donaldson, his editor at Futura, could sample Ismail's skills. Among the many people who know him, Ismail's reputation in the kitchen is already a legend.

The arrangement was that apart from providing the setting I would prepare some basic ingredients. At the "pre-arranged" hour of 7:15–7:30 Ismail was due to appear with his ingredients. By 8:00, no Ismail and unknown guests due to appear any minute. At 8:10 the bell tore through my nervousness and with trepidation I opened the door: Ismail, adorned with overflowing plastic bags and a rare and beautiful Kashmir shawl, rolled in wreathed in smiles. And so to cook.

By 8:45 the assembled guests were smiling, tantalized by the delicate aromas wafting about the rooms. Old friends such as Madhur Jaffrey, Terence Stamp, Ravi and Caroline Misra, and Raimond Buitons could fantasize with some authenticity on the work of the thirty-five-minute magician in the kitchen. Uninitiated, Anthony Smith of the British Film Institute, Edward Adeane of Palaces Royal, and Nicole Mackey of Rank Films could imagine less precisely what elusive surprises were in store. By playing cook's assistant for twenty to thirty minutes, I had hoped to cull some secrets, but Ismail's nimble fingers and improvisations were too quick, so even for me each dish had its own delicate surprise.

Since that meal, when I invite close friends to dinner, they very often ask me whether or not Ismail will be cooking. There is a distinct note of disappointment on those occasions when I say no. I have even overheard some of these same close friends offering freshly caught trout to Ismail—not to me—for our next "joint" Albany dinner!

—*Sarah Fox-Pitt*

My Idea of Giving the Perfect Dinner Party: Ismail Cooks

Out of the blue, during the summer of '84, Ismail phoned to say he was in town. "Let's meet at your place for dinner, let's all meet," he enthused, as dinner for Ismail always seems to include as many people as possible.

"Oh, Ismail," I wailed, "I'm in rehearsal all day and won't be home until at least six-thirty. There's no food in the fridge," and similar lame excuses.

"Don't worry," he said. "I'll cook!"

I got back from work tired and dusty, leapt in and out of the bath, fluffed a few cushions, and put out some peanuts. At 6:45, I opened my door to a beaming Ismail bearing four bulging carrier bags containing what would be dinner for the masses—surely he had invited many more by now.

For the twenty or more years I've known him, Ismail has always managed, remarkably, to fit in shopping for beautiful food in between meetings and filming. In the old days when we were all younger and poorer, Ismail would turn up with even the salt and pepper and the odd pound of butter just in case we didn't have any in stock. This evening he had bought fresh fish, mushrooms, bread, garlic, fresh herbs and spices, green beans, salad ingredients, and the rice he's so fond of, basmati. He made himself at home in the kitchen with a glass of cold white wine and with great panache set to, flourishing a knife, chopping garlic and onions. He has a genius for walking into a kitchen, any kitchen, bustling about for half an hour, and producing a feast fit for the gods, never having to ask where the oil is kept or anything so mundane as that.

The guests arrived, mostly family and close friends. We sat looking at the rose garden, watching the Thames, and sipping our wine, while smells of fabulous food came from the kitchen. In twenty minutes Ismail had everything under control and joined us. That evening we were a particularly happy group of people. Ismail was in town with Jim Ivory, and Dick Robbins was with them. Also with us were my sister Jennifer, her daughter Sanjana, and Michael, my husband.

The meal was a triumph and, as always, there was a fight over the last green bean and the last magnificent mushrooms. Eating Ismail's food causes people to forget their usual manners when it comes to the last available bites. That evening was typical of the many meals we have shared together in different houses and in different countries. It ended with a walk in the garden, coffee, chocolates, and a lot of laughs. There was a feeling of happy togetherness, with no hassles, the hostess having done nothing but provide the kitchen and a few pots and pans. It was a magical occasion, like many in the past and, I hope, many to come and all because Ismail said, "I'll cook!"

—*Felicity Kendal*

"Guess Who's Coming to Dinner"

"Who? Ingrid Bergman? Ismail, are you serious!" My mind didn't race, it began to shriek. What should I cook? Who else should come? Oh God, you mean *here* this evening!? I began to rage, "Ismail, you are joking. How can I be expected to prepare?" I tailed off as Ismail's warm, soothing, Bombay-clad voice gently eased me back to earth.

"Ruth and Ava Jhabvala are also coming and Ingrid's agent, Kay Brown, a wonderful New Yorker—and of course I'll be there," as if that would solve everything. "At eight, then. I'll do the cooking, so go and get . . ." he continued, giving me a surprisingly short list of ingredients, nothing extraordinary— pretty simple, really.

I spent all day rehearsing: "How do you do, Miss Bergman." No, too formal. "Hi, Ingrid, welcome to the Korners." No, too informal. And deciding what to wear: fincry and formal or free and freaky. And nervous about meeting this high-powered agent from New York; she sounded formidable. Oh, if only I had read English literature at least.

The day raced past. The ingredients were bought and laid out and chores were all done.

Six-thirty passed: no Ismail. Seven P.M.: nerves stretched to breaking point and still no Ismail. At 7:05 the phone rang. "Ismail, where are you?" Soothing excuses didn't work this time. "Get over here," I said with venom.

He arrived cool as the Indian guru from *Bombay Talkie*. The chickens were stuffed with mushrooms, ginger, and parsley. Lemon juice was squeezed over them and the squeezed peel stuffed inside. Mustard was painted over and the birds thrown in the oven. The peas were organized and rice put in pots, everything done in ten minutes. Ismail suggested we go upstairs and have a drink and I weakly asked, "That's all?"

Ingrid and Kay arrived punctually at eight, Kay carrying her own bottle of whiskey, "knowing Ismail well," she explained. The evening was marvelous, the food Ismailishly delicious, and Kay and the lovely Ingrid were star guests.

—*Sandra Korner*

3

Hors d'Oeuvres and Drinks

Here I include some recipes for drinks (alcoholic and nonalcoholic) and for some Indian-inspired hors d'oeuvres.

With regard to alcohol, I generally do not serve much more than white wine or cold beer when I invite guests. Over the years, my friends who wanted whiskey often had to bring their own bottle. When I remember to have it around, I do, otherwise I don't worry. It seems to me that spirits dull all the senses, and I want the taste buds to remain fully receptive to what I have in store for them. Even so, I admit that on a hot summer day, a gin and tonic can be a delight. . . .

Mustard and Chive Prawn Bites
Rai aur Piyaz Chingri Chat

This is an hors d'oeuvre I concocted for two of my food- and cookery-loving friends, Jeannie and Allen Miller.

Preparation and cooking time: about 20 minutes *Serves 6–8*

- **2 pounds raw prawns, defrosted if frozen**
- **3 bay leaves, crumbled**
  Salt
- **3 tablespoons snipped chives, or 1 tablespoon freeze-dried chives**
- **2 tablespoons Dijon mustard**
- **¼ teaspoon cayenne pepper**
- **4 tablespoons lemon juice**

Shell and clean the prawns.

Heat a saucepan of water with the bay leaves to the boil. Salt it generously and add the prawns. Cook for 1–1½ minutes, drain, then refresh them immediately in cold running water. Drain well and pat the prawns dry on paper towels.

Mix the chives, mustard, cayenne pepper, and lemon juice together.

Stir the mixture into the well-drained prawns and serve skewered on cocktail picks.

Deep-Fried Cheddar Balls
Paneer Bhajya

Preparation and cooking time: about 25 minutes   *Serves 6–8*

 8 ounces Cheddar cheese, finely grated
 2 large eggs
 2 tablespoons chick-pea (gram) flour
 ¼ teaspoon baking powder
 1 green chile, seeded (optional) and chopped
 2 teaspoons chopped coriander leaves
 ¼ teaspoon salt
   Vegetable oil for deep frying
   Tomato chutney, to serve

Mix the cheese, eggs, flour, baking powder, chile, coriander leaves, and salt thoroughly. If the mixture is too wet, add in a little more flour; if it is too dry, mix in a little beaten egg white.

Form the mixture into teaspoonfuls and put them aside on a dish.

Heat the oil in a deep-fat fryer or in a saucepan to a depth of about 2 inches until it is quite hot. Carefully transfer the cheese balls to the hot oil and cook, in batches if necessary, until they are golden.

Drain the balls on paper towels and serve them hot and skewered on cocktail picks; good with Tomato Chutney (page 229).

Bombay Vegetable Fritters
Bambai Bhajya

Preparation and cooking time:　　　　　　　　　*Serves 6–8*
letting the batter rest 30 minutes, plus about 30 minutes

- 1 small cauliflower, cut into bite-size florets
- 2 medium-size onions, thickly sliced and divided into rings
- 2–3 medium-size potatoes, boiled until just tender, then cooled under cold running water, drained, peeled, and cut into bite-size rounds
  Vegetable oil for deep frying

For the batter
- 2 teaspoons vegetable oil
- 6 ounces chick-pea (gram) flour
- 1½ teaspoons salt
- 1 teaspoon ground cumin
- 1 teaspoon ground coriander
- ½ teaspoon cayenne pepper

First make the batter. Rub the oil into the flour until the oil is evenly absorbed. Mix in the salt, cumin, coriander, and cayenne pepper.

Slowly pour in 1 cup warm water, beating continuously until the mixture is thin and smooth. A food processor or electric blender does this admirably.

Let the batter stand for about 30 minutes. Meanwhile prepare the vegetables.

Heat the oil in a deep-fat fryer or in a large saucepan to a depth of about 2 inches. When it is quite hot, dip the vegetables into the batter, shaking off the excess, and fry them in batches until they turn golden brown.

Drain them on paper towels and serve them hot, with cocktail picks.

Fresh Sardine Snacks
Taze Sardine ki Chat

Preparation and cooking time: *Serves 6–8*
1–2 hours marinating, plus 20 minutes

   Juice of 2 lemons
4 tablespoons Dijon mustard
1 teaspoon dried tarragon
1 pound fresh sardines, cleaned
   Vegetable oil for frying

Whisk the lemon juice, mustard, and tarragon together.

Lay the sardines in one layer in a nonmetal dish and pour over the lemon juice mixture. Leave the sardines to marinate for 1–2 hours, turning them in the marinade occasionally.

Heat oil to a depth of about ½ inch in a frying pan over medium-low heat. When hot, shake the excess marinade from the sardines and transfer them carefully to the oil. Reduce the heat, partly cover, and fry the fish gently for 10–15 minutes, turning them occasionally.

Drain the sardines on paper towels and serve them warm or at room temperature with cocktail picks for skewering.

Sweet Lassi
Meethi Lassi

Preparation time: *Serves 6*
10 minutes, plus chilling (optional)

3¾ **cups plain yoghurt**
 ½ **cup rose water**
 4 **tablespoons sugar**
 1 **dozen shelled, unsalted pistachios, coarsely chopped**

Whisk all the ingredients with 3¾ cups water for 3–4 minutes until the mixture becomes frothy.
    Serve at room temperature or chilled.

Salty Lassi
Namkeen Lassi

Preparation time: *Serves 6*
10 minutes, plus chilling (optional)

3¾ **cups plain yoghurt**
 ½ **teaspoon salt**
 ½ **teaspoon ground cumin**

Whisk together all the ingredients with 3¾ cups water for 3–4 minutes until the mixture becomes frothy. Correct the seasoning and serve at room temperature or chilled.

A Better Gin and Tonic

Preparation time: 5 minutes   *Serves 1*

    Ice cubes
2 ounces superior dry gin
    Freshly squeezed juice of ½ lemon or lime
    Tonic water
    Slice of lemon or lime to garnish

Fill a tall glass with ice cubes and add the gin.

Add the lemon or lime juice and fill the glass with tonic water.

Add the lemon or lime slice, and serve.

Vodka with Soda or Tonic and Mint

I suggest that this be enjoyed in a hammock. Do not try to navigate after drinking.

Preparation time: 5 minutes   *Serves 1*

    Ice cubes
  2 ounces 100 proof vodka
8–10 fresh mint leaves
    Soda or tonic water

Fill a large wine goblet with ice cubes and add the vodka.

Add the mint leaves, stir them vigorously, fill the glass with soda or tonic water, and serve.

Beer and Lemon
for a Hot Afternoon

This is a very satisfying drink for a sultry day.

Preparation time: 5 minutes   *Serves 1*

Ice cubes
10 ounces lager beer
Freshly squeezed juice of ½ lemon
Sprig of mint, to garnish

Fill a tall glass with ice, then add the beer.
    Stir in the lemon juice, insert the mint, and serve.

4

Soups

*J*ames Ivory, the director and my collaborator for many years, is a soup specialist who has inspired several of these recipes. He makes really exceptional soups, and goes about making them with great care, cutting and chopping so that the ingredients all look just right. I, on the other hand, am far more casual about the appearance of my soups, briskly chopping away with far less attention to detail. We may make films but not soup together, for collaboration is not good when making a soup. A soup should be the result of one cook, and one cook alone, as the saying goes, so try not to collaborate. There is rarely ever agreement about the right amount of salt, for example, when two parties season the cooking soup.

One of my favorite lunches—any time of the year—is a really terrific soup, an exceptional salad, very fresh bread served hot, and a glass of good wine or beer. It is a superb menu for anybody. My soups are both hearty and spicy, with an Indian touch I hope you will enjoy.

Broccoli and Lemon Gazpacho
Broccoli aur Nimboo ka Shorba

This is one of the recipes being discussed during the dinner party in my film *Jane Austen in Manhattan,* when Anne Baxter's pearls fall into the soup.

Preparation and cooking time: 40 minutes, plus chilling   Serves 6

1½ pounds fresh broccoli, cut into bite-size florets
  2 tablespoons butter
  1 large onion, peeled and chopped
6¼ cups chicken stock
    Peel of ½ lemon
    Juice of ½ lemon
 10 large garlic cloves, peeled and chopped
1¾ cups light cream
    Salt

Reserve a few of the broccoli florets for a garnish and lightly steam the rest of the florets. Do not overcook, in order to retain color and crispness. Remove the florets from the pan and let them cool.

Melt the butter in a large saucepan over medium-low heat, add the onion, and cook until it begins to brown, stirring occasionally.

Add the broccoli, stock, lemon peel and juice to the pan. Raise the heat until the soup barely simmers, turn the heat to low, cover, and cook 15 minutes, until the lemon is soft.

Put the soup, in stages, through a food processor or blender, along with the uncooked garlic. Add the cream and salt to taste. Cool and chill the soup.

Garnish the soup with the reserved broccoli florets to serve.

Indian Gazpacho

Hindustani Gazpacho

One can make gazpacho out of all sorts of things. Virtually any raw vegetables will do, provided they have some crispness. Here is a very tangy version that requires no cooking.

Preparation time: 20 minutes, plus chilling　　　　　　*Serves 6*

- 6 large tomatoes, blanched and skinned
- 1 large onion, preferably red
- 1 large green or red pepper
- 2 bunches of radishes, trimmed
- 3 large carrots
- 3 large celery ribs
- 2 medium-size cucumbers, unpeeled
- 2 hot green chiles, seeded (optional)
- 6–8 large garlic cloves, peeled
- 2 tablespoons olive oil
- ½ cup tomato purée
- 6¼ cups chicken stock
- 1¾ cups dry red wine
- Salt

Chop all the vegetables and mix them in a large container with the chiles, garlic, olive oil, tomato purée, chicken stock, and red wine.

Put the mixture, in stages, through a food processor or blender. Do not let the soup become too thin, but make sure there are no chunks of unprocessed vegetables. Add salt to taste and chill before serving.

Ginger Broccoli Soup

Adrak Broccoli Walla Shorba

Preparation and cooking time: 25 minutes   *Serves 4*

    1 tablespoon butter
    1 medium-size onion, halved and finely sliced
3¾ cups chicken stock
2½ cups water
    1 inch piece of fresh ginger root, grated
    ½ teaspoon cayenne pepper
       Juice of 1 lemon
    ¾ pound fresh broccoli, cut into bite-size florets

Melt the butter in a saucepan over medium-low heat, add the onion, and cook until it begins to brown, stirring occasionally.

Meanwhile, heat the stock, water, and grated ginger in a saucepan for 5–6 minutes. Do not boil.

Add the onion, cayenne pepper, lemon juice, and then the broccoli to the liquid. Cook over medium heat, stirring occasionally, for 7 more minutes. Do not let the soup boil. Serve right away.

Hot Rough Tomato Soup
Tez Tamatar Shorba

You can add pasta to this soup toward the end of cooking. I suggest 2 tablespoons of pastina, tiny specks of pasta that can be added to the soup for 10 minutes before serving.

Preparation and cooking time: about 1¼ hours   *Serves 6*

  3 large or 6 medium-size ripe tomatoes
  2 tablespoons butter
  1 large onion, peeled and coarsely chopped
  1 small potato, diced small
  ¾ cup tomato purée
7½ cups chicken stock
    Pinch of thyme
  2 small dried chiles, seeded (optional) and chopped
  6 cloves
12 peppercorns
  3 bay leaves, crumbled
    Salt

Drop the tomatoes in boiling water to cover and remove the pan from the heat. After 1 minute, remove each tomato in turn and peel away the skin. Cut the tomatoes into rough chunks.

Melt the butter in a large saucepan over medium-low heat, add the onion and cook until it begins to turn golden, stirring frequently and reducing the heat if necessary.

Add the tomatoes to the onion with the potato, tomato purée, chicken stock, thyme, chiles, cloves, peppercorns, bay leaves, and salt to taste.

Simmer the mixture gently for 45 minutes to 1 hour.

Claverack Carrot Soup
Claverack ka Khas Gajar Shorba

This is a variation on potage Crécy.

Preparation and cooking time: about 1 hour   *Serves 4–6*

- 4 tablespoons unsalted butter
- 1 pound carrots, peeled and thinly sliced
- 1 large onion, peeled and chopped
- 2 large potatoes, peeled and coarsely diced
- 2 inch piece of fresh ginger root, peeled and grated
- 3¾ cups chicken stock
-    Salt
- 1¼ cups light cream

Melt half the butter in a small pan over low heat, add the carrots, stir, cover, and cook until they soften, stirring occasionally.

Meanwhile, melt the rest of the butter in a large saucepan over low heat, add the onion, and cook until it is soft, stirring occasionally. Remove the pan from the heat.

Add the carrots with the pan juices to the onions with the potatoes, ginger, and chicken stock. Bring the mixture to a boil, reduce the heat, and simmer for 30 minutes.

Add salt to taste. If the soup is too thick, add a little water or stock. Stir the cream into the hot soup and serve.

Note: As the ginger creates a tangy flavor like pepper, pepper is not necessary. For those who particularly like ginger, double the amount.

Avocado and Tomato Soup

Avacado aur Tamatar ka Shorba

Preparation time: 15 minutes, plus chilling　　　　　Serves 2–3

  3 medium-size ripe avocados
1¼ cups vegetable or chicken stock
  ½ cup cream
1–2 teaspoons grated, strained onion juice
  ½ cup tomato purée
1½ teaspoons lemon juice, or to taste
    Salt and pepper

Remove the seeds and skin from the avocados. Mash the flesh in a large bowl.

Whisk in the stock, cream, onion juice, tomato purée, and lemon juice.

Season with salt and pepper and, if wished, more lemon juice, and chill before serving.

Note: If you eliminate the tomato purée you will have a paler and milder-tasting soup, but the flavor of the avocados will become more prominent.

Hearty Soup
Dilkhush Shorba

What makes this soup distinctive is the ginger and dill, though the other ingredients, both fresh and leftover, may be varied according to what is found in the refrigerator. For example, chicken or sausage may be substituted for beef.

Preparation and cooking time: 35 minutes   *Serves 4–6*

> 2 tablespoons butter
> 3 medium-size carrots, thinly sliced
> 2 small onions, peeled and chopped
> 6¼ cups beef or chicken stock
> 6–8 ounces boneless roast beef, finely diced
> 1 large potato, diced small
> 1 inch piece of fresh ginger root, grated
> 2 tablespoons chopped fresh dill, or 2 teaspoons dill weed
> 1 medium-size red pepper, sliced into slender pieces
> 6 garlic cloves, peeled and chopped
> Pinch of chili powder
> ½ teaspoon salt

Melt the butter in a large saucepan over medium-low heat, add the carrots and onions and cook until the onions begin to brown, stirring occasionally.

Add the stock to the pan with the meat, potato, ginger, dill, half the pepper, garlic, chili powder, and salt. Bring the liquid to a boil, then reduce the heat and simmer gently for 20–25 minutes, or until the potatoes are very tender.

Correct the seasoning, stir in the rest of the pepper slices, and serve.

Sorrel Soup
Soral Shorba

My friend Joanna Rose visits me in Claverack, New York, and we spend time together there in my vegetable and herb garden discussing and debating the merits of each plant. She is very knowledgeable about many things, and also a good cook. She suggested this recipe for sorrel soup.

Preparation and cooking time: *Serves 4*
preparing the sorrel, plus 30 minutes

  2 **tablespoons butter**
¾ **cup sorrel leaves, trimmed and washed**
  5 **cups chicken stock**
  1 **ounce fresh or frozen, defrosted green peas, puréed**
  3 **egg yolks**
½ **cup light cream**
  4 **tablespoons chopped fresh chervil, or 1 tablespoon dried**

Melt the butter in a saucepan over low heat. Add the sorrel and cook 4–5 minutes, or until the leaves wilt, stirring occasionally.

Remove the pan from the heat, add the chicken stock and pea purée and put the pan over medium heat.

When the liquid is hot but not too close to boiling, remove it from the heat. Beat the egg yolks into the cream and stir them into the soup.

Put the pan over medium-low heat and stir gently until the soup thickens slightly, but do not let it boil. Sprinkle chervil over the top and serve.

Note: To serve cold, stir in ¾ cup sour cream instead of the pea purée, cream, and egg yolks.

Red Lentil Soup
Masoor Dal Shorba

Preparation and cooking time: about 30 minutes   *Serves 6*

   3 tablespoons vegetable oil
   1 medium-size onion, peeled and chopped
  12 peppercorns
   4 bay leaves, crumbled
  3¾ cups chicken stock
   ½ pound masoor dal (split red lentils), picked over,
      washed, and drained
   2 tablespoons chopped fresh parsley
   3 dry red chiles, seeded (optional)
      Salt
 ¼–½ inch piece of fresh ginger root, grated

Heat the oil in a large saucepan over low heat. Add the onion and cook until it begins to soften, about 5 minutes, stirring occasionally.

Add the peppercorns and bay leaves and cook 5 minutes longer.

Add the chicken stock, 1 cup water, the drained red lentils, parsley, chiles, and salt to taste. Cook over medium heat, stirring occasionally, for 10 minutes.

When the soup begins to boil, add the grated ginger. Continue cooking for another 10 minutes, or until the lentils are very soft, and serve.

Potato Watercress Soup

Aloo aur Hari Pati ka Shorba

Preparation and cooking time: about 1¼ hours　　　　*Serves 6*

      4 large potatoes
      4 tablespoons butter
      2 medium size onions, peeled and chopped
   3¾ cups chicken stock
      4 large garlic cloves, peeled and chopped
1–1½ teaspoons freshly ground white pepper
      1 bunch of watercress, stems removed
        Salt
   2½ cups milk

Cover the potatoes with water in a saucepan and boil until very tender, with the skins on or off, as you prefer, 15–20 minutes. The skins are healthy and good, and the soup will look agreeably speckled if you leave them on. Drain the potatoes.

Meanwhile, melt the butter in a large saucepan over low heat. Add the onions and cook until they soften but do not color, 8–10 minutes. Remove from the heat.

Add the chicken stock to the onions with the garlic, potatoes, and pepper. Bring to a simmer and cook for 25 minutes. Sprinkle the watercress on top of the simmering liquid without mixing in, and continue cooking for another 5 minutes.

Purée the mixture in a food processor or blender, in stages if necessary. Season with salt. Return to the saucepan.

Add the milk and heat the soup until it is very hot but does not boil, then serve.

Note: To serve this soup cold, simply stir the milk into the puréed mixture, cool, and chill. Serve the soup garnished with fresh watercress leaves or with about 3 peeled thinly sliced garlic cloves scattered over the top.

Fresh Mushroom Soup
Taza Kumbhi ka Shorba

Here is a very rich, delicious soup, but it is so filling that it might be unwise to begin a heavy meal with it. The soup is rather Middle-European in style, and one might ask what it's doing in this cookbook, but I concocted it with local ingredients in my kitchen in Claverack, New York.

Preparation and cooking time: about 1 hour   Serves 6

4–6 tablespoons butter
  1 large onion, peeled and chopped
  1 pound button mushrooms, washed and sliced
1¼ cups dry red or white wine (I prefer red)
3¾ cups chicken stock
1¾ cups heavy cream
    Small bunch of fresh parsley, finely chopped

Melt 2 tablespoons of the butter in a small frying pan over medium-low heat, add the onion, and cook 2–3 minutes, stirring frequently. It should not become too soft. Remove from the heat.

Heat another 2 tablespoons butter in a large saucepan over medium-low heat, add the mushrooms, and cook them 8–10 minutes, adding more butter as needed.

When the mushrooms are soft, add the wine and cook the mushrooms for 5 more minutes.

Add the chicken stock and onion to the mushrooms and simmer gently for 15 minutes over a low flame. Do not let the mixture boil.

Coarsely purée the mixture in batches in a food processor or blender.

When ready to serve, reheat the mushroom mixture, turn the heat to low, and stir in the cream. When hot but not boiling, serve the soup garnished with a sprinkling of parsley.

White Gazpacho Soup
Safaid Gazpacho Shorba

My friend Phyllis Parker gave me this recipe and I am proud to share it with you.

Preparation and cooking time: *Serves 6 8*
about 1 hour, plus cooling if wished

- 2 tablespoons butter
- 1 large onion, peeled and chopped
- 2 large cucumbers, peeled and thinly sliced
- 6¼ cups chicken stock
- Leaves of 3–4 fresh mint sprigs, plus extra to garnish (optional)
- 4 tablespoons ground almonds
- 1¾ cups light cream
- Salt

Melt the butter in a frying pan over medium-low heat, add the onion and cook until it just begins to brown, stirring frequently.

Add the cucumbers to the pan and cook over low heat for 2–3 minutes, stirring frequently. Do not let them brown. Add more butter if necessary.

Put the chicken stock, onion, and cucumber in a large saucepan, heat to a simmer, then reduce the heat to low, cover, and cook for 20 minutes.

Add the mint to the mixture and put it through a food processor or blender.

Whisk the ground almonds and cream into the mixture. Season with salt.

Reheat but do not boil the soup, or cool and chill and serve it as a cold soup. If the latter, reserve some small sprigs of mint as a garnish.

5

Fish

Bombay, the capital of the state of Maharashtra, is a great port, so there is a great deal of fishing in the area. My father and I would regularly go to Nul Bazaar to buy fish. This section of the market had fish stalls with marble slabs and wicker baskets underneath. The marble slabs would rest on the wicker baskets and the fish, freshly caught by the Maharashtra women, would lie in rows on top of the marble. The fisherwomen were ready to clean and scale the fish, cut it into pieces with their very sharp knives, and prepare it for the customer. They argued and gestured, trying to catch the attention of those strolling through the market. There were 100–125 fisherwomen sitting very closely together, with each stall about two steps apart. The women would have pomfrets, striped bass, sea bass, mackerel, prawns, tiny shrimps, fresh "Bombay Duck" (really a fish), and occasionally lobsters and crabs. I learned to recognize a good fish from a bad fish by pressing the head of the fish near the gills. If the fish is fresh, a white substance will form at the gill openings. If a red liquid forms, the buyer should beware: the fish is not fresh.

At the bazaar there was always great haggling over the prices of fish as there were no signs to tell us what the prices were. Fish were sold singly, in pairs, in fours, or tens or whatever you wanted; but you would always have to haggle with the fisherwomen, and great rows would occur with occasional screaming and shouting, just as fishwives are said to do. If you looked shocked at the price they asked for the fish, you could offer them twenty percent or twenty-five percent lower. The fisherwomen would then say nasty words to you such as, "Move on to the next stall! I have fish that only a connoisseur would buy and you are not that person." This phrase would be said by practically every fisherwoman in the bazaar. "You are not a connoisseur of fish, and my fish is only for the connoisseur!"

My father knew how to deal with these women. He would ask for a particular fish, usually pomfret, a lovely diamond-shaped fish and a favorite in Bombay. The women would bring out a wonderful pair of pomfrets. My father would never argue, as his reputation was that he would pay the top rupee for good fish, and he was never sold anything which was not the best quality. He was always offered the fish that had just been brought in to the market, because he frequented the stalls of two or three of his favorite fisherwomen. They expected him and would keep their best fish aside for him. Even if someone else came and offered them more money, they would keep the fish for him because of his reputation for buying the best. He actually ended up often paying much less than other customers!

Fish was prepared in our home with lots of coconut and fresh tamarind, which is yellow-green in color, and dark tamarind, which is brown, almost black. The dark tamarind gives a sour taste but it is wonderful with pomfret and coconut sauce. With the fish, we always had Kichri (see page 187), a dish made with a particular kind of lentil (toor dal; see page 197) and rice. This fish dinner was served with homemade mango pickle, and with poppadums baked on charcoal as opposed to a cooker. This would be a great meal in the afternoon, particularly in the monsoon season when an abundance of pomfrets was available in the market.

In my fish recipes there are lots of variations I have tried with mustard, coriander, and coconut. I have also combined ingredients such as dried French herbs and lemon with the fish. I have prepared fish baked, grilled, and cooked on top of the stove. I enjoy fish enormously. I think that it is one of the most healthy things you can eat, and it's also one of the best tasting. I can never understand someone who says, "I don't like fish"; I think that a person misses half of the enjoyment of food if he can't appreciate fish. Fish roes are also delicious, and I have included a recipe for them in the book.

Curried Fish in Yoghurt
Dahi-Walli Machli

Preparation and cooking time: 25 minutes   *Serves 4–6*

- ¾ cup vegetable oil
- 1½ pounds boned, skinned turbot, salmon, or other firm-fleshed fish, cut into large bite-size pieces
- 2 large onions, peeled and grated
- 8 garlic cloves, pressed
- 1½ inch piece of fresh ginger root, grated
- 1 teaspoon cumin seeds
- ¼ teaspoon turmeric
- 1 teaspoon chili powder
- 1 cup plain yoghurt
- ½ teaspoon salt
- 1 teaspoon sugar
- ⅛ teaspoon saffron powder

Heat ½ cup of the oil in frying pan over medium heat. When hot, fry the pieces of fish until they are lightly browned on all sides. Drain and reserve them.

Add the rest of the oil to the pan and fry the onions over medium-low heat until they begin to turn golden. Add the garlic, ginger, cumin, turmeric, and chili powder and fry for 2 minutes.

Add the yoghurt, salt, sugar, and saffron; bring to a boil, lower the heat, and simmer gently for 10 minutes.

Add the fish, cover, and cook for 2–3 minutes to heat it through. Serve immediately with Basmati Pilaf (page 191).

Ismail's Spicy Fish Roe
Masaledar Machli ke Unde

Preparation and cooking time: 25–30 minutes   *Serves 6*

   2 pounds cod roe in one piece
 ¼ teaspoon salt
   4 tablespoons vegetable oil
   1 teaspoon cumin seeds
1½ teaspoons freshly ground black pepper
   3 tablespoons Dijon mustard
 ½ cup lemon juice
   2 teaspoons fresh dill

Bring a large saucepan of water almost to the boil. Carefully add the roe with the salt, let the water come just to the boil, then lower the heat to a simmer.

   When the roe begins to become firm (10–15 minutes), remove it from the water, draining in a colander.

   Place the drained roe in a bowl, mash it well, and reserve.

   Heat the oil in a frying pan over medium-low heat. Add the cumin seeds and black pepper and fry them for 30 seconds.

   Stir in the mustard, then the roe, lemon juice, and dill and cook for 5–10 minutes. Serve warm.

Mackerel in Coconut Sauce
Naryal Machli ka Salan

Preparation and cooking time: *Serves 6*
making the coconut sauce, plus 20 minutes

2–3 large mackerel or bluefish (4–5 pounds in all),
    cleaned, discarding head and tail
1¾ cups Spicy Coconut Sauce (page 53)

Cut the fish into steaks of even thickness.
    Add the coconut sauce to a saucepan and bring to the boil.
    Add the fish steaks and simmer gently over lowered heat for
5–8 minutes, or until done. Serve with plain boiled rice.

Lobster in Spicy Coconut Sauce
Seepdar Machli aur
Naryal ka Salan

This is a heavenly dish, worth the trouble and expense, and
you can cook up to eight lobster tails in the same amount of
sauce by adding a little more hot water with the bay leaves.

Preparation and cooking time: *Serves 4*
making the coconut sauce, plus 20 minutes

    4 tablespoons vegetable oil
    1 teaspoon black mustard seeds
    4 bay leaves
2½ cups Spicy Coconut Sauce (page 53)
    4 lobster tails

Heat the oil in a large, deep saucepan over medium-low heat. Add the mustard seeds and let them cook for 1 minute.

Add the bay leaves and coconut sauce and simmer over medium heat for 5 minutes.

Add the lobster tails and simmer gently for 5 minutes, until the flesh is firm but not overcooked. If bought already cooked, just heat them through.

Serve the lobster with Basmati Pilaf (page 191) or Saffron Pilaf (page 189).

Spicy Coconut Sauce

Masaledar Naryal Salan

Preparation and cooking time: *Makes about 5 cups*
about 50 minutes

1 **coconut**
1 **medium-size red pepper, seeded, cored, and chopped**
6 **garlic cloves, peeled and chopped**
6 **tablespoons chopped parsley**
2 **tablespoons freshly ground black pepper**
1 **teaspoon salt**

Heat the oven to 400°F.

Bake the coconut for 15 minutes.

Place the hot coconut on concrete or another hard surface and smash it open with a hammer.

When the coconut pieces are cool enough to handle, peel away the brown papery skin from the white meat with a potato peeler. Chop any large pieces, if necessary, into smaller ones.

Put the coconut meat and the rest of the ingredients and ¾ cup water in a food processor or blender, in batches and with a little extra water if necessary, and liquefy the mixture.

Thin the coconut mixture with about 4 cups water.

Spicy Fried Pompano
Masaledar Tale Pompano

In India, this dish is usually made with pomfret, a delicious fish found in the ocean around Bombay.

Preparation and cooking time: *Serves 2*
15 minutes seasoning the fish, plus 15 minutes

> 4 pompano, each about 8 inches long, cleaned and
> defrosted if frozen
> Vegetable oil for frying
> ½ cup dried bread crumbs

For the masala paste
> 1 teaspoon chili powder
> ½ teaspoon turmeric
> 4 tablespoons chopped parsley
> 4 tablespoons vinegar
> 6 tablespoons Dijon mustard
> 1 teaspoon freshly ground black pepper
> ½ teaspoon salt

Mix the ingredients together for the masala (spice) paste. Cover the fish with the paste and leave for 15 minutes.

Fill a deep frying pan with about 1 inch of oil and let it heat over a medium heat. Meanwhile, coat the fish in the breadcrumbs, shaking off the excess.

When the oil is hot, fry the fish for 8–10 minutes, turning once, in batches if necessary, until the crumbs are nicely browned. Serve right away with crusty French bread and a green salad.

Spicy Coconut Prawns
Naryal Chingri Masaledar

Preparation and cooking time:
making the masala, plus 15 minutes

Serves 4

- ½ cup mustard oil
- 4 bay leaves, crumbled
- 1 medium-size onion, peeled and chopped
- 1 pound shelled raw shrimp, cleaned
- ¼ teaspoon salt
- 12 cherry or 6 small tomatoes, quartered

For the masala

- Meat of 1 fresh coconut, broken into small pieces (page 53)
- 6 garlic cloves
- 1½ inch piece of ginger root, cut into 2–3 pieces
- 5–6 green chiles, seeded (optional)
- 1 tablespoon chopped fresh parsley
- 4 tablespoons vinegar
- 4 bay leaves

Combine the masala ingredients in a food processor for about 2 minutes and reserve.

Heat the oil in a small frying pan over low heat. When hot, add the bay leaves and onion and cook, stirring occasionally, until the onion softens.

Add the masala, stir and cook for 2–3 minutes.

Add the shrimp and cook for 1 minute, stirring all the while.

Add the salt and tomatoes, cover, and continue cooking for 3–4 minutes. Stir and serve with plain boiled rice.

Mackerel Sautéed with Mustard and Dill

Rai aur Suwa ki Bhuni Machli

Preparation and cooking time: about 15 minutes   *Serves 4–6*

3¾ pounds mackerel, cleaned, discarding head and tail
  Juice of 2 large lemons
 5 tablespoons Dijon mustard
 4 large garlic cloves, peeled and chopped
 4 bay leaves, crumbled
 ½ teaspoon cayenne pepper
 ½ teaspoon salt
 ½ cup vegetable oil
4–5 tablespoons chopped fresh dill

Cut the fish across into steaks, each about 1½ inches thick.

Combine the lemon juice, mustard, garlic, bay leaves, cayenne pepper, and salt in a bowl, then add the mackerel steaks and stir to coat them.

Heat the oil in a frying pan over low heat, add the mackerel, and sauté it gently for 10–12 minutes, turning once, or until the fish is done.

Sprinkle with the dill and serve with Green Pea Pilaf (page 186).

Baked Mackerel and Tomatoes

Tamatar Walli dum Machli

Preparation and cooking time: 25 minutes   *Serves 4–6*

3¾ pounds mackerel, cleaned, discarding head and tail
  ¼ cup vegetable oil
  1 tablespoon caraway seeds
12 cherry or 6 small tomatoes
  ¼ cup vinegar
  ¼ teaspoon salt
  1 teaspoon chili powder

Cut the fish across into steaks, each about 1½ inches thick.

Heat half the oil in a large frying pan over low heat. Add the caraway seeds and cook for 3–4 minutes.

Add the mackerel steaks, then place the tomatoes on top of the fish.

Combine the vinegar, the rest of the oil, salt, and chili powder and pour the mixture over the fish and tomatoes. Cover and cook over low heat for 15 minutes, or until done. Serve with Yellow Turmeric Rice (page 192).

Baked Red Snapper
Dum ki Lal Machli

Preparation and cooking time: about 1 hour   *Serves 3–4*

2½ pounds red snapper, cleaned
4 tablespoons lemon juice
1 tablespoon caraway seeds
1 hot green chile, sliced and seeded (optional)
   Salt and freshly ground black pepper

Heat the oven to 350°F.

Place the fish in a greased baking pan. Sprinkle over 2 tablespoons of the lemon juice, then sprinkle over half the caraway seeds, half the sliced chile, and a pinch each of salt and pepper.

Turn the fish over and repeat with the rest of the ingredients. Bake for 45 minutes. Serve with Cashew Rice (page 194).

Note: You can substitute smaller whole firm-fleshed fish in this recipe, such as mackerel.

Grilled Halibut
Machli ka Tikka

This is my favorite way to cook halibut, and it also produces delicious results with other flatfish such as turbot and haddock.

Preparation and cooking time: about 25 minutes   *Serves 5–6*

- ¼ cup lemon juice
- 3 pounds halibut steak, about 1½ inches thick, sliced into serving portions
- 3 tablespoons chopped parsley
- ½ teaspoon freshly ground black pepper
  Pinch of salt
- 3 garlic cloves, peeled and thinly sliced
- 3–4 parsley sprigs, to garnish
- 3–4 lemon slices, to garnish

Heat the broiler. Rub the lemon juice into the fish.

Coat both sides of the fish with parsley, pepper, salt, and garlic. The garlic will adhere if sliced thin enough.

Place the fish in a foil-lined, then greased baking pan. When ready, place the fish about 7 inches from the broiler heat and cook for 8 minutes.

Turn the fish over and continue cooking for 8 minutes, or until the fish is done but not dry and overcooked.

Garnish with parsley sprigs and lemon slices and serve with Chile-Tomato Salad (page 178).

Pan-Braised Haddock
Tali Hui Machli

Preparation and cooking time: 15–20 minutes   *Serves 2–3*

¼ cup olive oil
1 tablespoon Dijon mustard
½ teaspoon cumin seeds
  Pinch of salt
2 bay leaves, crumbled
¼ teaspoon freshly ground black pepper
2 pounds haddock, salmon, or other fish steaks
2 garlic cloves, peeled and thinly sliced

Combine the olive oil, mustard, cumin seeds, salt, bay leaves, and black pepper.

Transfer the mixture to a large frying pan over medium heat, then add the fish steaks in one layer

Add the garlic slices and ¾ cup hot water. Cover the pan and cook over medium-low heat for 10–12 minutes, or until the fish flakes easily with a fork but remains moist. Serve with Green Pea Pilaf (page 186) and a mixed salad.

Baked Trout in Mushroom Vinaigrette

Kumbhi Dam ki Machli

Preparation and cooking time: 45 minutes   *Serves 3–4*

- ¼ pound mushrooms
- 1 tablespoon Dijon mustard
- 2 tablespoons vinegar, lemon juice, or dry sherry
- 1 tablespoon vegetable oil, plus extra for greasing and basting
- 3–4 trout, each about ¾ pound, cleaned
- ½ teaspoon freshly ground black pepper
- ¼ teaspoon salt

Heat oven to 350°F.

Place the fish and mushrooms in a greased baking pan. Whisk together the mustard, vinegar, and oil and pour the mixture over the trout and mushrooms.

Sprinkle over the pepper and salt and bake for 20 minutes, basting with a little extra oil, until the fish is done. Serve with plain boiled rice.

Baked Stuffed Carp
Shikampur Machli

Preparation and cooking time: about 30 minutes　　　*Serves 4*

4 pounds carp, cleaned
6 scallions, finely chopped
2 garlic cloves, finely chopped
¼ cup lemon juice
¼ teaspoon salt
2 tablespoons chopped parsley
½ teaspoon cayenne pepper
12 cherry or 6 small tomatoes

Heat the oven to 350°F. Stuff the fish with the scallions and garlic.

Place the fish in a foil-lined, greased baking pan and cover both sides of the fish with lemon juice, salt, parsley, and cayenne pepper.

Place the fish in the oven for 10 minutes.

Place the tomatoes around the fish and bake another 10–15 minutes. Serve with Cardamom and Coriander Rice (page 185).

Note: As an alternative, striped or silver mullet can be substituted for carp in this recipe.

Fish Pilaf
Machli ka Pullao

Preparation and cooking time: 30–35 minutes　　　　*Serves 4–6*

2 tablespoons vegetable oil
1 medium-size onion, peeled and chopped
8 cloves
2 garlic cloves, peeled and chopped
½ teaspoon salt
　Pinch of turmeric
1¾ cups long-grain rice
1 pound cod, salmon, turbot, plaice, or similar fish fillets cut into bite-size pieces
4 small tomatoes

Heat the oil in a large saucepan over medium-low heat. When hot, add the onion and cook, stirring occasionally, until it softens but does not brown. Add the cloves, garlic, salt, turmeric, and 3 cups water. Bring to a boil, add the rice, and lower the heat to a simmer. Cover and cook until the water is almost all absorbed, about 15 minutes.

Add the fish and tomatoes, stir, cover, and cook for 5–8 minutes, or until the rice and fish are cooked. Serve right away.

Note: Leftover cooked fish can be used in this dish, too, by adding the fish when the rice is ready and off the heat. Stir in the fish, cover, and let it heat through for 2–3 minutes before serving.

Mustard Shrimp
Sarson-Walla Jhingha

Preparation and cooking time: 15 minutes   *Serves 4*

- ¼ cup vegetable oil
- ½ teaspoon caraway seeds
- ½ teaspoon chili powder
- 1 pound raw shrimp, shelled, cleaned, washed, and dried
- 1½ tablespoons Dijon mustard
  Pinch of salt
- ¼ cup lemon juice

Heat the oil in a small frying pan over low heat. When hot, add the caraway seeds and chili powder and cook for 3–4 minutes.

Add the shrimp, mustard, salt, and lemon juice and stir well. Cover the pan and cook for 5–6 minutes.

Stir the mixture well and serve with Saffron Pilaf (page 189) and a green salad.

Baked Sea Bass
with Cumin and Tomatoes

Zeera aur Tamatar-Walli Rawas

Preparation and cooking time: 30–40 minutes   *Serves 6*

   ½ cup Dijon mustard
   ¼ teaspoon salt
   4 garlic cloves, cleaned and chopped
   1 tablespoon cumin seeds
4–6 pounds sea bass, cleaned
  12 cherry or 6 small tomatoes

Heat the oven to 325°F. Combine the mustard, salt, garlic, and cumin seeds.

Place the bass into a foil-lined, greased baking pan and pour the mustard sauce over it. Add the tomatoes, cover, and bake for 20–30 minutes, or until the fish is done but not over-cooked and dry. Serve with lemon wedges and Basmati Pilaf (page 191) or new potatoes.

Yoghurt Shrimp
Dahi-Walla Jhingha

Preparation and cooking time: 15 minutes　　　　*Serves 6*

- ¼ cup vegetable oil
- 4 garlic cloves, chopped
- 1 tablespoon ground cumin
- 1 tablespoon chili powder
- ¼ teaspoon salt
- 24 raw jumbo shrimp, shelled, cleaned, washed, and dried
- 1 cup plain yoghurt

Heat the oil in a frying pan over medium-low heat. When hot, add the garlic, cumin, chili powder, and salt and cook for 5 minutes, or until the garlic begins to brown.

Add the shrimp and cook for 2–3 minutes, stirring.

Add the yoghurt, stir, and continue cooking for 5 minutes. Serve with Raw Spinach Salad (page 181).

Shrimp with Mustard and Dill

Rai-Walla Jhingha

Preparation and cooking time: Serves 6–8
cleaning, then marinating the prawns, plus 10 minutes

2 pounds raw shrimp, shelled, cleaned, washed, and
  dried
1 cup Dijon mustard
2 teaspoons cayenne pepper
2 garlic cloves, finely chopped
1 teaspoon caraway seeds
¼ teaspoon turmeric
  Salt
¼ cup vegetable oil
1 large bunch of fresh dill, finely chopped

Combine the mustard, cayenne pepper, garlic, caraway seeds,
turmeric, and salt to taste. Add the shrimp and blend well.
Cover and refrigerate for at least 1 hour and up to 6 hours.

Heat the oil in a deep frying pan over medium-low heat.
When hot, add the shrimp, shaking them to remove most of
the marinade. Stir well, cover, and cook for 3–4 minutes, or
until they just become firm.

Sprinkle over the dill and stir it in well, then serve the
shrimp right away with boiled rice and the remaining marinade as a sauce.

Spicy Fish Curry
Machli ka Salan

Preparation and cooking time: 20–25 minutes   *Serves 4–6*

1½ pounds cod or other white fish steaks, skin removed
    About 6 tablespoons vegetable oil
  2 large onions, peeled and halved, then sliced thin
 ½ teaspoon ground coriander
 ¼ teaspoon turmeric
  1 teaspoon chili powder
 ½ teaspoon ground ginger
  6 garlic cloves, pressed or very finely chopped
  1 large tomato, chopped
 ½ teaspoon salt
 ½ cup plain yoghurt
  1 teaspoon sugar

Cut the fish into large bite-size pieces. Heat 3 tablespoons of the oil in a frying pan over medium heat. When hot, add the pieces of fish and lightly brown them quickly on all sides, adding a little more oil if necessary. Remove the pan from the heat; remove the fish from the pan and reserve.

Heat 3 tablespoons of oil in the same pan over medium-low heat and when hot, cook the onions until they are light brown, stirring occasionally.

Add the coriander, turmeric, chili powder, ginger, and garlic and cook for 2–3 minutes.

Add the tomato and salt and cook until the tomato is soft, adding 1 tablespoon water at a time if the spices stick. Stir in the yoghurt and sugar and simmer gently for 5 minutes.

Add the fish, stir in well to heat through, and serve immediately with plain boiled rice.

Note: This curry is also good with mackerel, salmon, haddock, or mullet.

Shrimp Pilaf

Jhingha Pullao

Preparation and cooking time: 50–60 minutes   Serves 6

1¾ cups basmati rice
 1 inch piece of fresh ginger root, grated
 4 green chiles, seeded (optional) and finely chopped
 1 teaspoon chili powder
 ¼ teaspoon turmeric
 ¼ teaspoon ground coriander
 8 garlic cloves, finely chopped
 ¼ cup lemon juice
 ¼ cup vegetable oil
 2 medium-size onions, peeled and chopped
 2 cinnamon sticks, broken into pieces
12 cloves
24 large shrimp, shelled, cleaned, washed, and dried
 4 tablespoons chopped parsley

Put the rice in a bowl and wash it in several changes of cold water. Cover it with plenty of fresh water and let it soak for 30 minutes.

Meanwhile, combine the ginger, chiles, chili powder, turmeric, coriander, garlic, and lemon juice to make a paste; reserve.

Heat the oil in a large, heavy-based saucepan over medium-low heat. When hot, add the onions, cinnamon, and cloves and sauté until the onion is beginning to brown, stirring occasionally.

Add the paste to the sautéed onion mixture with ¾ cup water and simmer for 8–10 minutes.

Add the shrimp and continue cooking over low heat for 2 minutes.

Remove the shrimp from pan with a slotted spoon and set them aside.

Add 2½ cups hot water to the spice mixture in the pan and bring it to the boil.

Drain the rice well, then add it to the pan, stirring well. Cover the pan very tight and cook over low heat for 15 minutes, or until the water is absorbed.

Remove the pan from the heat, stir the reserved shrimp into the rice, cover, and let the shrimp finish cooking in the heat of the rice for 5–10 minutes.

Sprinkle with the parsley and serve.

6
Poultry and Eggs

*C*hicken has always been one of my favorite dishes. When I was a little boy my father would take me to the bazaar where there would be twenty or thirty chickens cooped up in large straw baskets. The chicken seller would greet my father and ask, "Would you like three or four today?" and my father would ask to see one first. The seller would pluck out one chicken from the straw basket, and all the other chickens would cluck and squawk. There was quite a din in the bazaar because other chicken salesmen would be picking birds out of their cages, too. The salesman would hold the chicken upside down by its legs and lift the wings up. The salesman would ask my father to feel how plump and meaty the breasts were. My father would then buy three or four chickens, which would be removed (screaming and carrying on) from the straw basket. We would then proceed to the part of the bazaar where the chickens would be slaughtered and left in a straw basket to drain. Then the chickens would be plucked and cut into pieces. This chicken expedition would occur twice a week, one of them usually on the weekend. I was always fascinated by the idea of picking out a chicken, examining it, seeing it slaughtered, brought home, and prepared. (Sometimes the chickens would even have a marvelous bag of eggs inside.) When I was a child, we didn't have a refrigerator, so everything was prepared fresh from the market and cooked the same day, except for pickles and chutneys. These were made in large quantities and sealed in jars so they would last a year or so.

If you have important guests for dinner in India, you serve chicken, almost as beef is served in the West for such occasions. Indians consider chicken a dish for the well-to-do. In India when my college friends would come home with me for dinner, I would always request several chicken dishes, including chicken biriyani made with basmati rice, saffron, yoghurt, ginger, garlic, fresh mint, and coriander. The combination of these ingredients created an extraordinary aroma, which we smelled while waiting for dinner.

When I go to buy chicken now, I still look for the same excitement I felt in the bazaar. Unfortunately I doubt that I can relive my childhood memories of chicken. I certainly don't relive them when I walk into a supermarket and see chickens which have been prepackaged months earlier in plastic and frozen. Once I went to a farmer near my home in New York and bought two fresh chickens. He slaughtered them in front of me and cleaned them, and with childlike excitement I brought them home and cooked them immediately. But it turned out that they were old roosters and so tough that they took a much longer time to cook than I could spare, and in the end I had to throw them both away.

Caraway-Cayenne Roast Chicken

Shazeera-Walla Murgh Mussallam

Preparation and cooking time: *Serves 4–6*
making the stuffing (optional), plus about 1½ hours

  1 chicken, about 3 pounds
  1 lemon
 ½ teaspoon salt
½–1 teaspoon cayenne pepper
  1 teaspoon caraway seeds

Heat the oven to 300°F. Squeeze the lemon over the chicken and place the rind in the chicken cavity (or fill cavity with stuffing—see pages 75–77). Sprinkle with salt and pepper, then with caraway seeds.

Place the bird in a greased baking pan and roast it for 1½ hours, or until done.

Serve with Lemon Lentils (page 198) and Raw Spinach Salad (page 181).

Chile-Ginger Roast Chicken
Mirch-Adrak-Walla Murgh Mussallam

Preparation and cooking time: *Serves 6*
making the stuffing, plus about 1 hour 20 minutes

    2 inch piece of fresh ginger root
2-(4) garlic cloves, peeled
    2 <u>hot</u> green chiles, seeded (optional)
    4 tablespoons vinegar
  ¼ teaspoon salt
    1 chicken, about 3 pounds
      Stuffing of your choice (see following recipes)
    1 tablespoon vegetable oil, plus extra for greasing

chop half

Heat the oven to 300°F. Grate the ginger and garlic and finely chop the chiles, then mix them with the vinegar and salt—or combine these ingredients in a food processor.

Stuff the chicken with one of the following stuffing mixtures, and place it in a greased baking pan. Rub the skin with the oil and spread the ginger and garlic mixture over the chicken.

Bake for 1½ hours, or until done. Serve with Pistachio Raita (page 175) and Kichri Rice (page 187).

Lemon, Ginger, and Chile Stuffing for Chicken

Nimboo Adrak aur Mirch ka Murgh Mussallam

Preparation and cooking time: *Enough for a 3-pound chicken*
5–10 minutes

2 green chiles, seeded (optional)
1 lemon, seeded and chopped
2 inch piece of fresh ginger root, peeled and chopped
¼ teaspoon salt
½ teaspoon freshly ground black pepper
1 cup dry bread crumbs
1 teaspoon caraway seeds

Combine the chiles, lemon, ginger, salt, and pepper in a food processor, or chop them together well.

Blend the bread crumbs and caraway seeds into the chile mixture.

Chile and Parsley Stuffing for Chicken

Mirch aur Kothmeer ka Masala

Preparation time: 5 minutes   *Enough for a 3-pound chicken*

- ½ cup yoghurt
- 2 dried red chiles, seeded (optional) and finely chopped
- ¼ teaspoon chili powder
- ¼ teaspoon salt
- 3 tablespoons chopped parsley
- 1 cup dry bread crumbs

Mix together the yoghurt, chopped chiles, chili powder, salt, and parsley.

Blend the bread crumbs into the mixture.

Pancakes and Chutney Stuffing for Chicken

Chilla aur Chutni-Walla Murgh

Preparation time: *Enough for a 3-pound chicken*
making the pancakes, plus 5 minutes

- 2 tablespoons spicy-hot chutney
- 1 inch piece of fresh ginger root, peeled and grated
- 1 green chile, seeded (optional) and chopped
- 5 tablespoons vinegar
- 1 teaspoon salt
- 1 cup fresh, cold pancakes torn into small pieces

Combine the chutney, grated ginger, chile, vinegar, and salt, then mix thoroughly into the pancakes.

Chopped Meat and Giblet Stuffing for Chicken

Qeema Masale-Walla Murgh

Preparation time: *Enough for a 3-pound chicken*
making the chopped meat, plus 5 minutes

1½ cups Chopped Meat with Peas Kashmiri-Style (page 126)
  1 inch piece of fresh ginger root, peeled and grated
  3 tablespoons vegetable oil
  1 teaspoon salt
    Giblets from the chicken, chopped
  1 green chile, seeded (optional) and chopped
  ½ cup wholemeal bread crumbs

Combine the chopped meat, ginger, vegetable oil, salt, chopped giblets, and chile. Add the bread and mix thoroughly.

Ginger Chicken
Adrak-Walli Murgh

Preparation and cooking time: 45 minutes　　　　　　*Serves 4*

- ¼ cup vegetable oil
- 1 chicken, about 3 pounds, cut into small pieces
- 2 medium-size onions, peeled and chopped
- 2 garlic cloves, peeled and chopped
- 2 cinnamon sticks
- 2 inch piece of ginger root, peeled and grated
- 1 pinch saffron in ¾ cup hot water
- 2 teaspoons freshly ground black pepper
- 1 teaspoon salt
- 4–6 small tomatoes
- 4 tablespoons vinegar

Heat the oil in a large heavy-based frying pan over medium-high heat, and when hot, add the chicken pieces. Turn them frequently until they are lightly browned on all sides, then remove them with a slotted spoon, shaking off the oil, and reserve the pieces.

Stir the onions, garlic, cinnamon, and ginger into the pan, lower the heat to medium, and stir frequently until the onions begin to brown, 5–7 minutes.

Return the chicken to the pan with the saffron-water and season with pepper and salt. Add the tomatoes and vinegar to the pan, cover, and cook over low heat for 20–25 minutes, or until the meat is very tender. Serve with Yellow Turmeric Rice (page 192).

Tandoori Chicken
Tandoori Murgh

At first Christopher Reeve seemed reluctant to try spicy cooking, but eventually he happily freed himself from being victim of the propaganda against Indian food. His other favorites besides Tandoori Chicken are Ginger Chicken (page 78), Spiced Okra (page 161), and Clove-Garlic Mixed Vegetables (page 150).

Preparation and cooking time: *Serves 4*
2 hours for overnight marinating, plus about 1 hour

2 inch piece of fresh ginger root, peeled and grated
4 garlic cloves, peeled and grated
1 teaspoon cumin seed
½ teaspoon cayenne pepper
¼ teaspoon salt
1 cup plain yoghurt
1 chicken, about 4 pounds, cut into serving pieces
2 tablespoons vegetable oil
½ teaspoon turmeric

Combine grated ginger, garlic, cumin seed, cayenne pepper, salt, and yoghurt.

Put the chicken pieces in a foil-lined baking pan, pour over the yoghurt mixture, and use your hands to coat the meat completely. Leave the chicken to marinate for at least 2 hours, or preferably overnight.

Heat the oven to 350°F. Dribble the oil over the chicken in the baking pan, and sprinkle the chicken with turmeric. Place the pan in the oven and bake for about 1 hour, basting frequently with the oil and yoghurt marinade at the bottom of the pan. Serve with hot pita bread and Lemon Lentils (page 198).

Chicken Breasts Sautéed with Chile and Cinnamon

Murgh Kabab

Preparation and cooking time: 25 minutes   *Serves 4–6*

¼ pound butter
1 large onion, peeled and chopped
1 cinnamon stick, broken up
8 boneless chicken breasts, cut in halves lengthwise
½ cup lemon juice
1 teaspoon salt
1 teaspoon freshly ground black pepper
1 green chile, seeded (optional) and chopped
4 tablespoons chopped parsley

Melt the butter in a heavy-based frying pan over medium-low heat. When hot, sauté the onion with the cinnamon until the onion begins to soften, 5–7 minutes, stirring occasionally.

Add the chicken breasts, lemon juice, salt, and pepper and continue cooking for 8 minutes, stirring occasionally.

Add the chile and parsley, lower the heat, and cook for another 8–10 minutes, until the meat is done.

Serve with Basmati Pilaf (page 191).

Yoghurt Chicken I
Dahi Murgh I

Preparation and cooking time: 1 hour 20 minutes   Serves 10–12

½ cup vegetable oil
2 medium-size onions, peeled and chopped
4 dried whole red chiles
12 cloves
5½ pounds chicken drumsticks and thighs
1 inch piece of fresh ginger root, peeled and grated
1½ cups plain yoghurt
1 teaspoon salt
1 tablespoon freshly ground black pepper

Heat the oil in a large heavy-based frying pan or saucepan over medium heat. When hot, add the onions, chiles, and cloves, and cook, stirring frequently, until the onions brown.

Add the chicken and ginger and stir continually until the meat is seared on all sides.

Mix the yoghurt and 1 cup water together and add them to the pan with salt and pepper. Cover and cook over medium-low heat, stirring occasionally, for 1 hour. Serve with Savory Onion Rice (page 190) and Dressed Green Salad (page 179).

Yoghurt Chicken II
Dahi Murgh II

Preparation and cooking time: 1 hour 20 minutes   *Serves 10–12*

- ½ cup vegetable oil
- 2 medium-size onions, peeled and chopped
- 1 bay leaf, crumbled
- 5½ pounds chicken drumsticks and thighs
- 2 teaspoons cumin seeds
- 1½ cups plain yoghurt
- 1½ teaspoons cayenne pepper
- 1 teaspoon salt
- 1 large tomato, quartered

Heat the oil in a large heavy-based frying pan or saucepan over medium heat. When hot, add the onions and bay leaf, and cook, stirring frequently, until the onions brown.

Add the chicken and cumin seeds and stir continually until the meat is seared on all sides.

Blend the yoghurt and ½ cup water together and add them to the pan with the cayenne pepper and salt.

Add the quartered tomato, cover, and cook over a medium flame, stirring occasionally, for 1 hour. Serve with Basmati Pilaf (page 191) and Pistachio Raita (page 175).

Chicken Korma
Murgh Korma

Preparation and cooking time: about 40 minutes   Serves 4–6

 ½ cup cooking oil
 2 medium-size onions, peeled and chopped
 4 whole dried red chiles
 2 cinnamon sticks, broken up
 6 cloves
 1 chicken, 2½–3 pounds, skinned and cut up
1¼ cups yoghurt
 ½ teaspoon salt
 4 tablespoons freshly ground black pepper
 1 pound fresh or frozen peas

Heat the oil in a large saucepan over medium-low heat. When hot, add the onions, chiles, cinnamon, and cloves, and cook, stirring frequently, until the onions brown.

Add the chicken pieces and stir frequently until the meat is seared on all sides.

Mix the yoghurt with 1¼ cups water and add this to the saucepan with the salt and pepper. Cover and cook over low heat for 20 minutes.

Add the peas, cover, and cook for 10 minutes longer.

Serve right away with Basmati Pilaf (page 191) and Tomato Mint Raita (page 180).

Spicy Mustard Chicken
Masale-Walli Rai Murgh

Felicity Kendal is always fond of this dish, which I prepare for her. She always asks for Lemon Lentils (page 198) and Cucumber Raita (page 140).

Preparation and cooking time: 1 hour   *Serves 6–8*

½ **cup vegetable oil**
2 **medium-size onions, peeled and chopped**
7 **cloves**
2 **chickens, about 2½ pounds each, cut through the bones into small pieces**
1 **teaspoon salt**
1 **teaspoon freshly ground black pepper**
½ **teaspoon chili powder**
2 **tablespoons Dijon mustard**
½ **cup tarragon vinegar**

Heat the oil in a large heavy-based frying pan or saucepan over medium heat. Add the onions and cloves and cook, stirring frequently, until the onions brown.

Add the chicken, salt, pepper, chili powder, mustard, vinegar, and 1¾ cups water.

Cook the mixture over low heat for 40–45 minutes, until the meat is tender. Serve with plain boiled rice and Chicory-Walnut Salad (page 178).

Chicken in Coconut Sauce
Naryal-Walla Murgh

Shashi Kapoor has always been a great eater and enjoyed many, many of my meals in Cannes, London, New York, Claverack, Hyderabad, and Bombay. Among his favorites are this chicken dish, Basmati Pilaf, (page 191), and Va-Va-Voom Potatoes (page 139).

Preparation and cooking time: *Serves 6–8*
preparing the coconut, plus 1¼ hours

> **Meat of ⅔ fresh coconut, in small pieces (see note)**
> **2 green chiles, seeded (optional)**
> **2 inch piece of fresh ginger root, peeled**
> **4 garlic cloves, peeled**
> **2 tablespoons lemon juice**
> **1½ teaspoons salt**
> **2 chickens, about 2½ pounds each, cut through the bones into small pieces**
> **½ cup vegetable oil**
> **2 medium-size onions, cut into quarters**
> **2 teaspoons freshly ground black pepper**

Coarsely purée the coconut, chiles, ginger, garlic, lemon juice, salt, and ½ cup water in a food processor or blender.

Place the chicken pieces in a large saucepan with the oil, onions, pepper, 1 cup water, and coconut purée.

Bring the liquid to a boil, then lower the heat and simmer gently for 1 hour, until the meat is tender. Correct the seasoning and serve with plain boiled rice.

Note: To remove the meat from a fresh coconut, bake it first in a 400°F. oven for 15 minutes. Place the hot coconut on concrete or other hard surface and smash it open with a hammer. When cool, peel away the brown paper skin with a potato peeler.

Tomato Chicken
Tamatar Murgh

Preparation and cooking time: about 1 hour   *Serves 6*

½ cup vegetable oil
1 large onion, peeled and chopped
1 cinnamon stick, broken into pieces
4 black cardamom pods
1 chicken, about 3 pounds, cut through the bones into
   about 10 small pieces
2 teaspoons caraway seeds
2 teaspoons freshly ground black pepper
½ teaspoon salt
4 large tomatoes, sliced
1 bunch fresh parsley, chopped

Heat the oil in a frying pan over medium heat and when hot, add the onion, cinnamon, and cardamom pods. Cook, stirring frequently, until the onion is brown, about 5 minutes.

Add the chicken, caraway seeds, pepper, and salt and cook, stirring, over medium-low heat for 15 minutes.

Add the tomatoes and chopped parsley, turn the heat to low, and cook, stirring occasionally, for 30 minutes, until the chicken is tender. Serve with Basmati Pilaf (page 191).

Pepper Chicken
Kali Mirch Murgh

Preparation and cooking time: 1–1¼ hours   *Serves 4*

½ cup vegetable oil
2 medium-size onions, chopped
7 black cardamom pods
1 teaspoon cumin seeds
1 chicken, about 3 pounds, cut into pieces
  Juice of 2 medium-size lemons
2 tablespoons freshly ground black pepper
2 tablespoons green peppercorn mustard
½ teaspoon salt
6 garlic cloves, peeled and pressed

Heat the oil in a heavy-based saucepan over medium heat. When hot, add the onions, cardamom pods, and cumin seeds and cook, stirring frequently, until the onions begin to brown.

Add the chicken pieces and cook, stirring frequently, for 10 minutes.

Combine the lemon juice, pepper, green peppercorn mustard, and salt with 1 cup water and pour the mixture over the chicken and onions. Let the mixture cook over medium-low heat for 15 minutes.

Add the garlic and continue cooking for 30–40 minutes, stirring occasionally, until the meat is tender; add a little more liquid if necessary to prevent burning. Serve with Basmati Pilaf (page 191) and Cucumber Raita (page 140).

Richard's Chicken
Richard ka Khas Murgh

Preparation and cooking time: 25 minutes   *Serves 4*

    2 tablespoons oil
    1 medium-size onion, peeled and chopped
    1 cinnamon stick, broken into pieces
    1 inch piece of fresh ginger root, grated
    4 boneless chicken breasts
  3–4 tablespoons Meaux or other coarse-grained mustard
    ½ teaspoon salt
    ½ teaspoon coarsely ground pepper
    ½ teaspoon cumin seeds
    ½ teaspoon turmeric
    3 tablespoons chopped parsley

Heat the oil in a frying pan over medium heat. When hot, add the onion, cinnamon, and ginger; cook, stirring frequently, until the onion browns.

Cut the breasts in half lengthwise. Spread mustard over them very generously. Salt and pepper them and add them to the frying pan with the onion.

Turn the heat to low and sprinkle cumin seeds, turmeric, and parsley over them. Cook for 7–8 minutes.

Turn the meat over, cover the pan, and cook 5 minutes longer, until the meat is done. Serve with Saffron Pilaf (page 189).

Note: A simple yet delicious sauce for chicken breasts can be made by gently heating ¼ cup each of coarse-grained mustard with heavy cream and pouring it over the sautéed meat.

Spicy Chicken Curry
Murgh Masala

While we were shooting *Quartet* in Paris, Maggie Smith succumbed to my Spicy Chicken Curry, served with Cashew Rice (page 194) and Spicy Stewed Cauliflower and Potatoes (page 153). Later I prepared my Mackerel in Coconut Sauce (page 52) for her during the shooting of *A Room with a View*.

Preparation and cooking time: 30 minutes   *Serves 4*

    3 tablespoons vegetable oil
    1 large onion, sliced
    6 peppercorns
    1 cinnamon stick
    4 cardamom pods
    6 cloves
    2 bay leaves, crumbled
    1 chicken, about 3 pounds, cut into pieces
    ¼ teaspoon turmeric
    ½ teaspoon chili powder
    ½ teaspoon ground coriander
    ½ teaspoon ground cumin
    ½ teaspoon ground ginger
      Salt
    2 garlic cloves, peeled and pressed
    ½ cup plain yoghurt
    ½ teaspoon ground allspice

Heat the oil in a large saucepan over medium heat. When hot, add the onion, peppercorns, cinnamon, cardamom pods, cloves, and bay leaves, cook, stirring frequently, until the onion becomes light brown.

Add the chicken pieces and cook, stirring frequently, until the meat is seared on all sides.

Sprinkle in the turmeric, chili powder, coriander, cumin, ginger, and salt to taste. Stir in the garlic. Continue cooking, stirring occasionally, until the chicken is well colored.

Add 1¾ cups hot water, cover, and simmer until the chicken is just cooked.

Add the yoghurt and allspice and simmer for 10 minutes. Serve with Green Pea Pilaf (page 186) and Cucumber Raita (page 140).

Chicken Livers Baked in Spicy Yoghurt

Dahi-Walli Murgh Kalejee

Preparation and cooking time: 50 minutes   *Serves 4*

1 cup plain yoghurt
1 teaspoon freshly ground black pepper
1 green chile, seeded (optional) and finely chopped
4 garlic cloves, peeled and chopped
¼ teaspoon salt
2 tablespoons softened butter
1 pound chicken livers

Combine all the ingredients except the chicken livers in a small ovenproof dish.

Add the chicken livers and marinate them for 15 minutes.

Heat the oven to 325°F. Place the dish in the oven and bake for 30 minutes, until the livers are done, basting frequently with the yoghurt sauce. Serve with Raw Spinach Salad (page 181) and Yellow Turmeric Rice (page 192).

Chicken Livers Baked in Spicy Mustard

Rai-Walli Murgh Kalejee

Preparation and cooking time: 50 minutes   *Serves 3–4*

⅓ cup plain or flavored Dijon mustard
1 teaspoon freshly ground black pepper
4 garlic cloves, peeled and chopped
2 tablespoons chopped parsley
1 teaspoon cumin seeds
2 tablespoons softened butter
1 pound chicken livers

Combine all the ingredients except the chicken livers in a small ovenproof dish.

Add the chicken livers and let them marinate for 15 minutes.

Heat the oven to 325°F. Place the dish in the oven and bake for 30 minutes, until the livers are done, basting frequently with the mustard sauce. Serve with Cashew Rice (page 194).

Roast Stuffed Duck

Bathak Mussallam

Preparation and cooking time: *Serves 2–3*
making the stuffing, plus about 2½ hours

1 oven-ready duck, about 5 pounds, with giblets
   Salt and freshly ground black pepper
   Stuffing (see following recipe)
2 garlic cloves, peeled and pressed

Heat the oven to 350°F. Wash the giblets and set them to simmer in water to cover for 20–30 minutes to make a rich stock.

Meanwhile, wash duck thoroughly, then dry it. Remove any visible fat from the neck and rear cavity.

Sprinkle salt inside the cavity, then fill it with stuffing and truss the duck (see note).

Rub with the pressed garlic and 1 teaspoon or more pepper. Prick the breasts with a fork to release the fat during cooking.

Place the bird on a trivet or rack in a roasting pan and roast for 2 hours, until the duck juices run clear. Baste often with the drippings and some of the giblet stock.

Serve the duck and stuffing with the rest of the warmed stock served separately. Serve with Watercress, Celeriac, and Chicory Salad (page 169) and roast potatoes.

Note: To truss the duck, pass a skewer through one wing of the duck, then through the neck flap and the other wing. Tie the legs together.

Ismail's Duck Stuffing
Khas Bathak Masala

Preparation time: 5 minutes   *Enough for a 5-pound duck*

3 tablespoons mustard
2 tablespoons vinegar
1 cup dried bread crumbs
1 hot chile, seeded (optional) and finely chopped
6 garlic cloves, peeled and chopped
1 apple, peeled, cored, and sliced
½ teaspoon salt

Combine the mustard and vinegar, and stir in the bread crumbs. Add the chile, garlic, apple, and salt.

Roast Stuffed Goose
Qaaz Mussallam

For Christmas 1983, we had a big crowd, so I prepared two geese. They aren't as difficult to cook as one might think—and they are delicious. They may make turkey seem rather bland by comparison.

Prepare the goose for roasting as you would a turkey, except you really must place it on a rack or trivet as it produces lots of fat while cooking. Prick the goose to release the fat during roasting.

Preparation and cooking time: *Serves 8–10*
making the stuffing, plus about 4¼ hours

1 **oven-ready goose, about 12 pounds**
   Salt
   Stuffing (see following recipe)
2 **tablespoons freshly ground black pepper**

Heat the oven to 325°F. Wash the goose thoroughly, dry it, and weigh it. Salt the inside, fill it with stuffing, and place it on a rack or trivet in a large roasting pan.

Prick the goose over the breast and legs. Sprinkle *lots* of ground black pepper over the goose.

Roast for 20–25 minutes a pound, checking from time to time to spoon off the excess melted fat. (Cool, then refrigerate this superbly flavored fat to use in cooking other dishes.)

Serve the goose and stuffing with roast potatoes and Dressed Green Salad (page 179).

Spicy Fruit Stuffing for Goose
Phal-Walli Qaaj Mussallam

Preparation time: 10 minutes   *Enough for a 12-pound goose*

- 1 cup dried bread crumbs
- 6 small whole crabapples
- 3 pears, peeled, cored, and coarsely chopped
- 1 cup raisins
- 1 tablespoon chopped parsley
- ½ cup mustard
  Salt
- 1 tablespoon cayenne pepper
- ½ pound potatoes, cooked and mashed
- ½ cup leftover Chopped Meat with Peas Kashmiri-Style (page 126), or chicken or goose giblets, chopped

Combine all ingredients in a large bowl.

Roast Stuffed Turkey
Feelmurgh Mussallam

In the United States my friends always want turkey for Thanksgiving. It's always good, but turkey can sometimes be rather bland, so I make a spicy dressing to increase the pleasure of roast turkey.

Preparation and cooking time: *Serves 12–16*
making the stuffing, plus 4¼–5¼ hours

1 **oven-ready turkey, 12 to 15 pounds, with giblets**
  Salt
  Stuffing (see following recipes)
  Freshly ground black pepper

Wash the giblets and simmer them in water to cover for 20–30 minutes to make a rich stock.

Heat the oven to 300°F. Wash the bird thoroughly, then dry and weigh it.

Rub inside with salt and fill with stuffing. Some cooks insist on sewing up the opening, but I am always in such a rush I don't have time.

Sprinkle with lots of black pepper, at least 1 tablespoon. To prevent the turkey from drying, cover it with cheesecloth moistened in the giblet stock to hold in the moisture.

Roast the turkey for 20 minutes a pound, basting frequently with the giblet stock.

Spicy Turkey Stuffing
Tez Feelmurgh ka Masala

As you use the giblets for this stuffing, baste the roasting turkey with olive or other vegetable oil.

Preparation time: *Enough for a 12 to 15 pound turkey*
10–15 minutes

   Turkey giblets, chopped
2 hot green chiles, seeded (optional)
2 medium-size onions, peeled and chopped
¼ cup tarragon vinegar
¼ cup olive oil
6 garlic cloves, peeled
3 tablespoons chopped parsley
4 dry red chiles, seeded (optional)
1½ cups dried bread crumbs
2 tablespoons chopped walnuts
2 tablespoons raisins

Combine giblets, green chiles, onions, tarragon vinegar, olive oil, garlic, parsley, and red chiles in a food processor.

Coarsely chop the mixture. Blend the bread crumbs thoroughly into the giblets mixture, then mix in the walnuts and raisins.

Ismail's Superb Turkey Stuffing
Khas Feelmurgh ka Masala

I added the first two ingredients to the bread crumbs because I found them in the refrigerator. I encourage you to also be *adventurous* in creating your stuffings.

Preparation time: *Enough for a 12- to 15-pound turkey peeling the chestnuts, plus 10 minutes*

  1 cup leftover cold Oxtail Dal (page 203)
 ¾ cup leftover Potatoes and Peas (page 138)
 ½ cup dried bread crumbs
  1 large onion, peeled and chopped
  2 green chiles, seeded (optional) and chopped
  2 teaspoons cumin seeds
  2 apples, peeled, cored, and chopped
24 chestnuts, peeled and chopped
 ½ cup vegetable oil
 ½ teaspoon salt
  1 teaspoon freshly ground black pepper

Combine all the ingredients, mixing thoroughly.

Tomato-Caraway Egg Curry

Tamatar Shazeera-Walla Rasedar Unde

Jennifer Kendal was a vegetarian, and though she never cooked she was nevertheless very discerning about Indian cuisine. She loved this egg curry and also Lemon Lentils (page 198) and Broccoli in Garlic-Lemon Butter (page 157). I enjoyed cooking for her.

Preparation and cooking time: *Serves 4*
hard-boiling the eggs plus 20 minutes

- 2 tablespoons vegetable oil
- 1 medium-size onion, peeled and chopped
- 4 bay leaves, crumbled
- 3 large tomatoes, chopped
- ¼ cup vinegar
- ½ teaspoon salt
- ½ teaspoon cayenne pepper
- ½ teaspoon caraway seeds
- 8 eggs, hard-boiled, shelled, and halved
- 4 tablespoons chopped fresh chives

Heat the oil in a saucepan over medium-low heat. When hot, add the onion and bay leaves and cook until the onion is tender, stirring occasionally.

Add tomatoes, vinegar, salt, cayenne pepper, and caraway seeds and simmer gently until the tomatoes are soft, about 10 minutes.

Add the halved eggs; cook 2–3 minutes to heat them through.

Sprinkle with the chives and serve with plain boiled rice, or warm pita bread.

Clove Curried Eggs
Long-Wale Rasedar Unde

Preparation and cooking time: Serves 4
hard-boiling the eggs, plus 25 minutes

- ¼ cup vegetable oil
- 2 medium-size onions, peeled and chopped
- 16 black peppercorns
- 8 cloves
- 3 bay leaves, crumbled
- 1 large potato, peeled (optional) and cut into medium-size dice
- ¼ teaspoon salt
- 2 tablespoons lemon juice or vinegar
- 2 teaspoons Dijon mustard, preferably lemon-flavored
- 8 hard-boiled eggs, shelled
- 1 tablespoon chopped parsley

Heat the oil in a saucepan over medium-low heat. When hot, add the onion, peppercorns, cloves, and bay leaves; cook, stirring occasionally, until the onion is tender.

Add the diced potato and salt to the pan with ¾ cup hot water. Whisk together the lemon juice or vinegar and mustard and stir them into the saucepan. Simmer the mixture gently for 15 minutes, until the potato is tender, adding a little more water if necessary.

Halve the eggs and add them to the pan with the parsley. Cook for 2–3 minutes and serve with Saffron Pilaf (page 189).

Ismail's Egg Salad
Ismail ka Unde Cachumber

Preparation time: Serves 4–6
hard-boiling the eggs, plus 10 minutes

10 hard-boiled eggs, shelled and chopped
 1 green chile, seeded (optional) and chopped
 4 scallions, chopped
 3 tablespoons mayonnaise
 1 tablespoon Dijon mustard
    Salt and freshly ground black pepper

Mix the ingredients together well and serve on lettuce leaves.

"Tortilla" Eggs with Parsley and Chile
Kothmiri Unde Roti

Preparation and cooking time: 10 minutes   Serves 2

4 medium-size eggs
1 tablespoon chopped parsley
1 small green chile, seeded (optional) and chopped
   Salt and freshly ground black pepper
2 tablespoons butter

Whisk the eggs with the parsley, chile, and salt and pepper to taste.

Melt the butter in a small frying pan over low heat. When hot, pour in the egg mixture. Cook the mixture, rather like a Spanish tortilla, for 5 minutes, until it is as firm as you like. Serve with a green salad dressed with olive oil and lemon juice.

Omelet Fines Herbes
Sookhi Patyoon ka Aam-Late

Preparation and cooking time: 10 minutes　　　　*Serves 2–3*

6 medium-size eggs
3 tablespoons butter
1 tablespoon fresh or 1 teaspoon dried fines herbes

Whisk the eggs together.

Melt the butter in a frying pan over low heat and add the whisked eggs.

When the eggs are *slightly* firm, sprinkle the herbs over them. After 3 minutes, use a spatula to turn half the omelet over onto the other half. Cook for 2 more minutes and serve with crusty bread.

Souffléed Scrambled Eggs
Khagina

Preparation and cooking time: 15 minutes　　　　*Serves 2–3*

2 tablespoons butter
1 medium-size onion, peeled and chopped
2 garlic cloves, peeled and chopped
¼ teaspoon cayenne pepper
1 green chile, seeded (optional) and chopped
2 small tomatoes, chopped
6 medium-size eggs
1 tablespoon chopped parsley

Heat the butter in a small frying pan over medium-low heat. When melted, add the onion and cook, stirring occasionally, until it begins to color.

Add the garlic, cayenne pepper, chile, and tomatoes, stirring.

Quickly whisk the eggs as if to scramble, and add them to the pan. Sprinkle with the parsley, cover, turn the heat to low, and cook for 10 minutes, until the mixture rises in the manner of a soufflé. Serve with crusty bread.

Scrambled Mustard Eggs

Rai ke Unde

Preparation and cooking time: 10–12 minutes   *Serves 4*

2 tablespoons butter
1 tablespoon Meaux or similar coarse-grained mustard
8 medium-size eggs
1 tablespoon cream
   Pinch of cayenne papper
   Pinch of salt

Melt the butter in a small frying pan over low heat. Add the mustard and cook for 3–4 minutes.

Whisk together the eggs with the cream, cayenne, and salt. Pour the mixture into the pan and stir. Cover and continue cooking for about 6 minutes, stirring occasionally. Don't let the eggs get too firm—they should be served soft. Serve with toast.

Ismail's Eggs
Khas Unde

Preparation and cooking time:
hard-boiling the eggs, plus 8–10 minutes

Serves 3–4

6 hard-boiled eggs, peeled and halved
2 tablespoons Dijon mustard
2 tablespoons wine vinegar
2 tablespoons olive oil
1 green chile, seeded (optional) and chopped
2 tablespoons chopped parsley
  Salt

Combine eggs, mustard, vinegar, olive oil, chile, parsley, and salt.

Cook over a low flame for about 3 minutes. Turn and cook 2 minutes longer. Serve immediately with crusty French bread.

7
Meat

As Muslims we are great meat-eaters, so meat was a part of our everyday cooking at home. It was served at our main meal, usually with some kind of *roti* (bread) and rice. We generally ate goat, the most common meat in India, except Kashmir, where lamb is more frequently cooked. There are no roasts in Indian cookery. Kebabs, on the other hand, are cooked frequently and eaten with great enjoyment and there are many, many recipes for them. Basically, a kebab is chopped meat combined with various flavorful ingredients and prepared in many ways. They can be meat patties cooked in a frying pan, or wrapped around a skewer and grilled over a charcoal fire in the same way as cubes of lamb, which are really another kind of kebab. There are also liver kebabs, kidney kebabs and ox tongue kebabs.

I have given recipes in this book for lamb roasts, rib roasts, and beef roasts, but the meat recipes I have created are usually not examples of traditional Indian cooking. In India, beef is eaten in restaurants and is prepared mainly in Muslim, Christian, and Parsi households and in the luxury hotels catering to foreigners. Beef in India comes mainly from water buffalo and bulls. Hindus, the majority of Indians, consider cows sacred and you will rarely see a Hindu eating a dish prepared from beef, except Westernized Hindus living in India or, more likely, outside the country.

In our household, beef was a great treat at home on Id-Uz-Zuha, a Muslim festival somewhat like the American Thanksgiving. Every Muslim family traditionally has to make a sacrifice on that day, of a cow, a camel, a goat, or a lamb. Naturally, more spiritual benefits are derived for the family from the slaughter of a large animal like a steer than from a mere goat. Fortunately nothing goes to waste in India; every part of the sacrificial animal is used in some way or another, rather in the same way as the thrifty French would do.

It is not essential to eat meat every day, though I have some friends who say they need it every day to give them energy and sustaining power for their creative work. Regardless of how often my friends enjoy meat, all of them agree with me that it should be tender and juicy, not cooked until it is falling apart or on the point of drying out. Whenever I bring a well-prepared, well-cooked roast to the table, I enjoy seeing the delight and satisfaction on the faces of my friends—and that, of course, is one of the very best reasons to cook.

Baked Lamb with Chile and Ginger

Dabba Gosht

Preparation and cooking time: about 1 hour   *Serves 6–8*

10–15 green chiles, seeded
    5 tablespoons vegetable oil, plus extra for greasing
    6 pieces fresh ginger root, each 1 inch, peeled and chopped
    2 pounds boneless lean lamb, cut in bite-size dice
      Salt

4 large tomatoes, coarsely chopped
1 large potato, boiled, peeled, and diced
3 tablespoons chopped coriander leaves
4 medium-size eggs

For the ground spice mixture
2 cardamom pods
2 cinnamon sticks, broken in pieces
6 cloves
½ teaspoon cumin seeds
8–10 black peppercorns

Purée the seeded chiles with 2 tablespoons of the vegetable oil in a food processor or blender and set aside.

Extract the juice from the pieces of ginger root by putting them through a garlic press. Reserve the juice and discard the pulp.

Put the lamb in a saucepan, cover with water, and bring to a boil. Immediately drain the meat in a sieve and discard the water. Rinse the lamb and return it to the pan with the chile purée and ginger juice.

Season the mixture with salt to taste, and add water just to cover. Bring the mixture to a boil, lower the heat, and simmer until the lamb is tender, about 30 minutes, adding more hot water as necessary.

Meanwhile, to make the spice mixture, grind the spices to a coarse powder in a mortar, food processor, or coffee mill.

Heat the oven to 375° F. When the meat is tender, raise the heat, rapidly boil off almost all the water, and remove the pan from the heat. Stir in the tomatoes, potato, coriander, and ground spice mixture.

Grease a small roasting pan and spread the lamb mixture inside. Beat the eggs well and pour them evenly over the mixture. Heat the rest of the vegetable oil until it is smoking hot, and immediately pour it over the lamb mixture. Bake for 15 minutes, until the eggs are set, then serve hot with warmed pita bread and Cucumber Raita (page 140).

Cubed Lamb with Mustard and Bay

Rai-Walla Boti Gosht

Preparation and cooking time: about 1 hour   *Serves 4–6*

½ cup vegetable oil
1 large onion, peeled and chopped
2 pounds boneless lean lamb, cubed
6 bay leaves, crumbled

For the sauce
½ cup Dijon mustard
2 teaspoons cayenne pepper
½ teaspoon salt
½ cup lemon juice
½ cup vinegar

Mix together the sauce ingredients and set them aside.

Heat half the oil in a large heavy saucepan over medium-high heat. When hot, brown the chopped onion quickly, stirring; remove with a slotted spoon and reserve.

Add the rest of the oil to the pan, and when hot, add the cubed meat, stirring it continually to brown it quickly on all sides.

Return the onion to the pan with the bay leaves, lower the heat to medium, and cook for 10 minutes, stirring occasionally.

Add the sauce to the meat mixture, cover, turn the heat to low, and cook for 35 minutes, until the meat is very tender. Serve with plain boiled rice.

Pan-Roasted Lamb
Bhuna Gosht

Preparation and cooking time: *Serves 12*
1 hour for marinating, plus 1¼ hours

1½ pounds boneless lean leg of lamb (about 7 pounds
     before boning)
  2 tablespoons finely chopped fresh ginger root
  3 hot green chiles, chopped with seeds
  1 tablespoon finely chopped garlic
1½ tablespoons chopped coriander leaves
     Juice of 1 lemon
     Salt to taste
  1 teaspoon freshly ground black pepper
  1 tablespoon vegetable oil

Cut the meat into 1½-inch cubes.

Place the lamb in a bowl, add the remaining ingredients, and mix them together. Set aside to marinate until you are ready to cook, but at least 1 hour.

Heat the oven to 350°F.

Put the lamb mixture in a shallow roasting pan about 16 × 9 inches. Bake, uncovered, 1¼ hours without stirring. The lamb should be tender with plenty of pan juices.

Serve with Basmati Pilaf (page 191) and a curly endive salad.

Rajasthani Spicy Lamb Stew
Rajasthani Gosht

Preparation and cooking time: 1¾ hours   Serves 4

 4 tablespoons vegetable oil
 1 pound boneless lean lamb, cut into 2-inch cubes
 2 medium-size onions, peeled and sliced
 1 inch piece of fresh ginger root, chopped
 8 garlic cloves, peeled and chopped
 1 teaspoon ground coriander
 ½ teaspoon ground cumin
 ½ teaspoon turmeric
 ½ cup plain yoghurt, stirred
 2 teaspoons chili powder
   Salt

Heat half the oil in a saucepan over medium-high heat. When hot, add the cubed lamb and stir constantly to brown on all sides. Remove the meat with a slotted spoon and reserve it.

Add the rest of the oil to the pan, and when hot, add the onions and brown them, stirring frequently to prevent burning.

Meanwhile, mix the ginger, garlic, coriander, cumin, and turmeric into the yoghurt. When the onions are browned, add the meat and yoghurt mixture to the pan, stirring. Reduce the heat to medium-low and simmer for 10 minutes, adding a little water if necessary to prevent burning.

Add the chili powder to the lamb, season with salt, and add 1¾ cups hot water. Cover, lower the heat, and simmer for 1¼ hours, until the meat is tender and the spicy gravy is thick. Serve with plain boiled rice.

COOKS.COM RECIPE SEARCH

LEFTOVER LAMB CURRY
Printed from COOKS.COM

```
1 apple, diced
1 onion, diced
4 tbsp. butter
Garlic powder to taste
1 to 2 tbsp. curry
1 tsp. ground ginger
1/4 tsp. pepper
2 c. chicken stock or 2 chicken bouillon in 2 cups water
1/2 c. raisins
3 c. cooked diced lamb
```

Saute apples and onion in butter. Sprinkle with all seasonings until soft. Add cornstarch. Gradually stir in chicken stock; add lamb and raisins. Simmer 30 minutes. Serves 4 to 6. Add at table, chutney's, coconut flakes, salted almonds, bacon bits, pineapple chunks.

Tomato Lamb Curry
Tamatar Gosht

Preparation and cooking time: about 1½ hours   *Serves 3–4*

- ¼ cup vegetable oil
- 3 bay leaves, crumbled
- 1 inch piece of cinnamon stick
- 4 cloves
- 4 cardamom pods
- 4 peppercorns
- 1 pound boneless lean lamb, cut into large bite-size pieces
- 1 large onion, peeled and grated
- ½ teaspoon ground ginger
- ½ teaspoon finely chopped garlic
- ¼ teaspoon turmeric
- ½ teaspoon ground coriander
- 1 teaspoon chili powder
- ½ teaspoon salt
- 1 large tomato, finely chopped
- 1 tablespoon chopped coriander leaves

Heat the oil in a saucepan over medium heat. When hot, add the bay leaves, cinnamon, cloves, cardamom pods, and peppercorns and cook until they begin to pop, 2–3 minutes.

Add the lamb and onion and cook, stirring, until the onion and the lamb are lightly browned.

Stir the ginger, garlic, turmeric, ground coriander, chili powder, and salt into the saucepan, turn the heat to medium-low, and cook for 3–4 minutes.

Add the chopped tomato to the mixture, stirring well, and cook for 5 minutes, until the tomato becomes very soft.

Add 1¾ cups hot water to the pan, bring to the boil, cover, and simmer over low heat for 1 hour, until the meat is tender. Stir in the chopped coriander leaves and serve with Basmati Pilaf (page 191).

Spicy Lamb Stew
Rogan Josh

Preparation and cooking time: about 1¼ hours   *Serves 4–6*

¼ pound butter
2 medium-size onions, peeled and chopped
1 cinnamon stick, broken up
6 cardamom pods
3 whole green chiles
6 garlic cloves, peeled and chopped
12 cloves
2 pounds boneless lean lamb, cut into large bite-size pieces
½ cup plain yoghurt
1 tablespoon coarsely ground black pepper

Melt the butter in a saucepan over medium-low heat. Add the onions and cook until soft, about 5 minutes, stirring occasionally.

Add the cinnamon, cardamom pods, chiles, garlic, and cloves and continue cooking for 8–10 minutes, stirring occasionally.

Add the meat and continue cooking for 4–5 minutes, stirring occasionally.

Stir together the yoghurt, ½ cup water, and pepper, then stir the mixture into the saucepan. Cover the meat and cook gently for 45 minutes, until tender. Serve hot with Green Pea Pilaf (page 186).

Roast Lamb with Ginger and Caraway

Adrak aur Shazeera-Walli Ran

Raquel Welch enjoyed this particular dish, which I prepared for her just before we began shooting *The Wild Party.*

Preparation and cooking time:　　　　　　　　*Serves 6–8*
1–2 hours marinating, plus about 2 hours

- 1 leg of lamb, about 7 pounds
  Salt
- 2 tablespoons chopped parsley

For the marinade
- ½ cup lemon juice
- 2 green chiles, seeded (optional)
- 6 dried red chiles, seeded (optional) and chopped
- 2 inch piece of fresh ginger root, peeled and chopped
- 1 teaspoon chopped parsley
- 1 tablespoon caraway seeds
- 3 large garlic cloves, peeled

Purée the marinade ingredients in a food processor.

Add salt to taste, then rub the marinade over the lamb on all sides. Leave the meat to season for 1–2 hours.

Heat the oven to 450°F.

Place the lamb and any marinade into a greased baking pan, sprinkle with the parsley, and cook in the oven for 30 minutes.

Reduce the heat to 400°F. and cook for 1 hour, or until done. Serve with warmed pita bread and Cucumber Raita (page 140).

Lamb with Onions and Tomatoes

Gosht do Piyaza

Preparation and cooking time: 45 minutes   *Serves 4–6*

- 1¼ cups vegetable oil
- 2 pounds onions, peeled and sliced
- 6 black cardamom pods
- 2 pounds boneless lean lamb, cut into large bite-size pieces
- 6–8 small dried red chiles
- 1 cup plain yoghurt
- 12 small whole tomatoes
- ½ teaspoon salt
- 1 tablespoon freshly ground black pepper

Heat the oil in a large heavy-based saucepan over medium heat. When hot, add the onions and cardamom pods and cook, stirring, until they are slightly browned. Remove them from the pan with a slotted spoon and drain them on paper towels.

Add the lamb and chiles to the hot oil in the pan and stir continually until meat browns on all sides, about 5 minutes.

Return the onions to the pan, turn the heat to low, and continue cooking for 10–15 minutes, stirring occasionally.

Add the yoghurt, tomatoes, salt, and pepper and cook over medium-low heat for another 15 minutes, until the lamb is tender. Serve with warmed pita bread and Tomato Mint Raita (page 180), telling people to avoid the cardamom pods and chiles if wished.

North Indian Lamb Chops
Dahi-Walli Chap

Preparation and cooking time: 40 minutes   *Serves 4*

1¾ cups plain yoghurt
½ teaspoon ground turmeric
1 teaspoon ground coriander
½ teaspoon salt
4 garlic cloves, peeled and finely chopped
½ cup vegetable oil
4 small dried red chiles
1 cinnamon stick, broken up
1 tablespoon black mustard seeds
8 lamb chops
4 tablespoons chopped fresh coriander

Mix the yoghurt, turmeric, ground coriander, salt, and garlic together in a bowl and reserve.

Heat the oil in a large saucepan over medium-low heat, and when hot, add the chiles, pieces of cinnamon stick, and mustard seeds. Let them cook for 4–5 minutes.

Add the lamb chops and cook them for 8–10 minutes, turning them halfway through.

Pour in the yoghurt sauce and continue cooking over low heat for 15–18 minutes, until the meat is just tender. Sprinkle the chopped fresh coriander or parsley on top and serve with Saffron Pilaf (page 189) and a simple raita made of beaten plain yoghurt.

Crown Roast of Lamb, Merchant-Style

Phasli ka Taj

Preparation and cooking time: *Serves 10*
45 minutes, plus roasting time

- 3 racks of lamb, each with 6–8 ribs, making a total of 20 ribs (2 per person)
  Juice of 1 lemon
- 1 tablespoon chopped parsley
- 1 teaspoon salt
- 1 teaspoon black pepper
- 1 inch piece of fresh ginger root, grated

For the stuffing
- ¾ pound chopped lamb (see below)
- ½ cup fresh white bread crumbs
  Juice of 2 lemons
- 4–5 spring onions, finely chopped
- ½ pound shelled fresh chestnuts, chopped, or canned unsweetened chestnuts, drained and chopped, or shelled walnuts
  Salt and freshly ground black pepper

Have the butcher cut away the skin from the racks, then trim the meat from the tops of the bones and have this chopped to use for the stuffing. Weigh the racks to calculate cooking time.

Then have the end bone of each rack sewed around, so that the racks are attached. Bend the racks round, stitching the ends together around the bones to form a crown. Tie the crown with kitchen string to hold the shape. Place the crown in a greased roasting pan.

Heat the oven to 300°F. Mix together some of the chopped

lamb with the rest of the stuffing ingredients to just fill the crown.

Combine the remaining ingredients and rub this evenly over the meat.

Roast for 30 minutes a pound and serve with a mixed curly endive salad.

Beef Rib Roast, Merchant-Style
Bhuna Phasli

Preparation and cooking time: *Serves 4*
marinating the meat, plus 2¼ hours

  4 pounds beef rib roast
    Freshly ground black pepper

For the marinade
  2 inch piece of fresh ginger root, peeled and chopped
  ½ cup lemon juice
  2 fresh chiles, seeded (optional) and chopped
  6 tablespoons chopped parsley
  ½ teaspoon coarsely ground black pepper

Place the beef on a plate or platter to fit inside the refrigerator. Generously grind pepper over the meat.

Put the marinade ingredients in a food processor or blender and process them into a paste. Spread the paste over the meat, cover well with plastic wrap, refrigerate, and leave to season for 4–24 hours.

Heat the oven to 350°F.

Transfer the beef to a greased roasting pan and roast for about 1½ hours for rare and 2 hours for medium. Serve with plain boiled rice and Cucumber Raita (page 140).

North Indian Beef and Eggplant Casserole

Shemali Gaye ke Tukre Baygan-Walla

Preparation and cooking time: 1 hour 20 minutes   *Serves 4*

      2 pounds boneless lean beef, chopped
 1½ cups plain yoghurt
      ½ teaspoon salt
      ½ teaspoon freshly ground black pepper
      5 tablespoons olive oil
      1 small eggplant, sliced
 8–9 small scallions
      1 green pepper, sliced
      1 large tomato, sliced
 4–5 dried red chiles, seeded (optional)

Heat the oven to 375°F. Combine the beef, half the yoghurt, half the salt and half the pepper in a 1-quart soufflé or similar-sized ovenproof dish greased with two tablespoons of the olive oil.

Slice the eggplant and spread the slices on top of the beef.

For the next layer, cover with the scallions, using the bulbs plus 3–4 inches of the green stems.

For the next layers, spread the sliced green pepper, then the sliced tomato over the scallions.

In a small bowl, mix together the rest of the yoghurt with the rest of the salt and pepper, and beat with a fork. Spread over to form the top layer.

Place the dried chiles on top and pour the rest of the olive oil over the whole dish.

Cover with a lid or foil and bake for 1½ hours. A substantial dish, serve it with a Raw Spinach Salad (page 181) or Chicory-Walnut Salad (page 178).

Cubed Beef with Scallions and Chiles

Hari Piyaz aur Mirch-Walli Boti

Preparation and cooking time: about 40 minutes   *Serves 4*

½ cup vegetable oil
1 medium-size onion, peeled and chopped
3 pounds boneless lean beef, cubed
2 teaspoons cumin seeds
1 cup lemon juice
4 garlic cloves
2 whole fresh green chiles, seeded (optional)
¼ teaspoon salt
2 teaspoons freshly ground black pepper
12 scallions, including 3 inches of green

Heat the oil in a large frying pan over medium heat. When hot, add the onion and stir continually until it turns golden, about 4 minutes.

Add the beef and cumin seeds to the pan and cook for 15 minutes, stirring occasionally and lowering the heat if necessary to prevent burning.

Add the lemon juice, garlic, chiles, salt, and pepper, and continue cooking for 10 minutes.

Add the scallions and cook another 10 minutes.

Serve with Lemon Lentils (page 198) and warmed pita bread.

Royal Kofta (Meatballs)
Shahi Kofta

Preparation and cooking time: 2½ hours   *Serves 8*

    2 pounds chopped lean beef
 1¼ cups plain yoghurt
 1½ teaspoons salt
    2 tablespoons finely chopped parsley
    1 inch piece of fresh ginger root, cut into small pieces
    5 green chiles, seeded (optional)
    6 garlic cloves
    4 tablespoons lemon juice
 1½ teaspoons cayenne pepper
   ¼ teaspoon turmeric
   ¼ teaspoon ground coriander
    1 cup vegetable oil
    3 medium-size onions, peeled and chopped
    6 bay leaves, crumbled
  12 cloves
    1 large pinch of saffron

Mix the chopped beef, ¼ cup of the yoghurt, 1 teaspoon of the salt, and the parsley together and set aside.

Combine the ginger, 3 of the chiles, garlic cloves, and half the lemon juice in a food processor to make a paste.

Transfer the paste to a bowl and add the cayenne pepper, turmeric, and ground coriander.

Place the meat mixture in a food processor and add the remaining lemon juice and 2 remaining chiles. Process until fairly fine.

Form the mixture into 1½-inch balls.

Heat the oil in a large, thick-bottomed saucepan. Brown the onions over medium heat, stirring, then add bay leaves and cloves.

The chef/film producer Ismail Merchant at home in his kitchen in upstate New York.

Ingredients in Indian sweets are nuts, fruits, and fresh milk or cream. Pictured are raisins, pistachios, cashews, almonds, and walnuts.

A sampling of spices and seasonings. The top thali contains, clockwise from the top, coriander seeds, turmeric, cayenne pepper, fennel seeds, whole black pepper, and mixed dried herbs, with cinnamon sticks and parsley in the center. The second thali contains, clockwise from the top, ground coriander, coarse ground pepper, cardomom pods, cumin seeds, red chili powder, black cardomom pods, and whole cloves in the center.

Late-night after-theater supper consisting of Spicy Red Cabbage, Basmati Pilaf, Lemon Lentils, and Chicken in Coconut Sauce.

A picnic in Claverack, featuring, clockwise from the flowers, James Ivory, Ismail Merchant, Sanford Allen, Madhur Jaffrey, Ruth Jhabvala, Richard Robbins, Diane Kagan, and Cyrus Jhabvala.

The Nawab's picnic from *Heat and Dust*.

James Mason and Madhur Jaffrey enjoy somosas, vanilla walnut cake, and tea in *Autobiography of a Princess*.

An arrangement of the simple, basic ingredients in Ismail Merchant's cooking.

Summer picnic at Claverack, New York. Tandoori Chicken is served with Coconut and Mint Chutney, Tarragon-Walnut Potato Salad, Mango Relish, and fresh cherries.

Winter's Sunday supper in the country, consisting of poppadums, Qeema garnished with tomatoes, Caraway-Onion Potato Salad, Beets Vinaigrette, and Spicy Stewed Cauliflower and Potatoes.

Verena Tarrant (Madeleine Potter) takes tea with Henry Burrage (John van Ness Philip) and Mr. Gracie (Peter Bogyo) in *The Bostonians*.

The Nawab's banquet from *Heat and Dust*.

Add reserved paste to the hot browned onions, together with 1¼ cups hot water and the rest of the salt; cook for 10–15 minutes over low heat. Add the rest of the yoghurt and cook for 5 more minutes.

Carefully add the meatballs to the sauce. They should be nearly submerged. Add the saffron.

Cover and cook slowly for 1½ hours. The meatballs should not break, but if some of them do, they will still taste fine. If you want to turn them, use a wooden spoon and do so gently.

Serve with Basmati Pilaf (page 191) and Lemon Lentils (page 198).

Baked Spicy Beefburgers
Chapli Kabab

This is my version of the hamburger. It is baked, rather than fried or grilled, and it is a bit spicier than the usual burger.

Preparation and cooking time: 40 minutes   *Serves 4–6*

1½ pounds lean chopped beef
  ¼ cup lemon juice
   2 medium-size eggs
   1 teaspoon cayenne pepper
  ½ teaspoon salt
   1 tablespoon finely chopped parsley

Heat the oven to 450°F. Mix all the ingredients together well and form the mixture into 4–6 patties.

Place them on a greased baking sheet and bake for 15–20 minutes.

Serve them with good mustard and bread.

Spicy Beef Potato Cakes
Qeema Aloo Tikki

Preparation and cooking time: about 1 hour　　　　　　　*Serves 4*

1 inch piece of fresh ginger root, peeled and chopped
4 garlic cloves, peeled and chopped
2 fresh green chiles, seeded (optional) and chopped
4 tablespoons finely chopped parsley
¼ cup lemon juice
½ teaspoon freshly ground black pepper
¼ cup vegetable oil
1 medium-size onion, peeled and chopped
8 cloves
1 pound chopped lean beef
3 large eggs
4 tablespoons butter

For the potato patties
4 large potatoes, boiled
1 tablespoon vegetable oil
¼ teaspoon salt
1 teaspoon cayenne pepper
2 tablespoons cream

Place the ginger, garlic, chiles, parsley, lemon juice, and pepper in a food processor or blender to make a "loose" paste. Reserve the paste. (This *hara masala,* or fresh green mixture, may be used to cook meat or chicken dishes. It is a fine all-purpose, very useful flavoring mixture).

Heat the oil in a large frying pan over medium-low heat. Add the onion and cloves to brown, stirring frequently.

Add the meat to the pan, stirring, to brown. After about 5 minutes, add the reserved *masala* paste. Cook over low heat for about 20 minutes, until the mixture is quite dry, stirring occasionally. Remove from the heat and reserve.

For the patties, peel the boiled potatoes, mash them with a fork, put them in a bowl, and mix in the oil, salt, cayenne, and cream. With your hands, make round patties about 3 inches in diameter and ¼ inch thick or less. The potatoes have to be well mashed so they will make fairly thin patties. A food processor may do the job well, but mashing by hand has worked well for centuries.

Place a portion of the dry beef mixture on one patty, place another patty over it, and pinch the edges together gently to join them, making a sort of meat-filled potato dumpling.

Beat the eggs together with a fork. Dip the patties into the beaten egg mixture to coat them, which also helps hold them together.

Melt the butter in a frying pan over low heat. Add the patties and fry them about 3 minutes on each side, turning once, until nicely browned. Serve with Tomato Mint Raita (page 180) and warmed pita bread.

Gingerburgers
Adrak-Walla Chapli Kabab

Here's another version of my hamburger with a surprise element of ginger.

Preparation and cooking time: 15–25 minutes   *Serves 4–6*

  1½ pounds lean chopped beef
  2 medium-size eggs
  ¼ cup plain yoghurt
  1 inch piece of fresh ginger root, grated
  1 green chile, seeded (optional) and finely chopped
  ¼ teaspoon salt
  1–2 garlic cloves, peeled and finely chopped

Heat the broiler. Combine all the ingredients thoroughly. Form the mixture into 4–6 patties and place them on the broiler pan or a baking sheet.

Broil about 10 minutes, turning once, for rare meat, about 15 minutes for medium, and 18–20 minutes for well done. Serve with your favorite mustard and good bread.

Chopped Beef with Potatoes
Aloo Qeema

Preparation and cooking time: about 50 minutes   *Serves 4*

¼ cup vegetable oil
3 medium-size onions, peeled and chopped
1 cinnamon stick, broken up
2 pounds chopped lean beef
2 large potatoes, peeled and cut into bite-size pieces
1 inch piece of fresh ginger root, grated
¼ cup plain yoghurt
1 large green chile, seeded (optional) and chopped
½ teaspoon salt
2 medium-size tomatoes, chopped

Heat the oil in a large frying pan over medium heat and brown the onions with the cinnamon.

Add the meat and stir continually until it begins to brown, 4–5 minutes.

Add the potatoes, ginger, yoghurt, chile, salt, and tomatoes.

Cover and cook over low heat for 40 minutes, until the meat is tender. Serve with plain boiled rice and Green Lentil Dal (page 200).

Note: You can add 1 cup fresh shelled or frozen peas, or fresh trimmed or frozen spinach in place of, *or* in addition to, the potatoes in the last 5–7 minutes of cooking.

Chopped Meat with Peas Kashmiri-Style

Kashmiri Qeema Mattar

Preparation and cooking time: 30–40 minutes   *Serves 2–3*

 1 pound chopped lean beef or lamb
  Salt
 ¼ teaspoon asafetida
 1 cup plain yoghurt, whisked
 1½ inch piece of fresh ginger root, grated
 ½ cup vegetable oil
 1 cup shelled peas, defrosted if frozen
 1½ teaspoons chili powder
 1 teaspoon ground coriander
 ½ teaspoon ground allspice
  Handful of chopped coriander leaves

Mix the meat, salt to taste, asafetida, yoghurt, and ginger together.

Heat the oil in a large frying pan over medium-low heat. Add the meat mixture, stirring occasionally to break up the meat.

When the mixture begins to dry out, add the peas, chili powder, ground coriander, and allspice and cook until the meat is well browned, stirring continuously to prevent burning.

Add 1 cup hot water, then gently simmer until the peas are cooked, about 10 minutes.

Remove the mixture from the pan with a slotted spoon, transfer to a serving dish, and stir in the coriander leaves. Serve with Cashew Rice (page 194) and Cucumber Raita (page 140).

Spicy Chopped Beef Kebabs
Motlabai Sheekh Kabab

Preparation and cooking time: about 20 minutes   *Serves 4*

2 tablespoons butter
1 large onion, peeled and chopped
3 garlic cloves, peeled and chopped
1 inch piece of fresh ginger root, chopped
1 teaspoon ground cumin
½ teaspoon ground cardamom
1 pound boneless lean chopped beef, lamb or pork
3½ tablespoons dry bread crumbs
1 beaten egg
3 tablespoons chopped mint leaves
1 green chile, seeded (optional) and chopped
¼ cup lemon juice
1 teaspoon salt
½ teaspoon cayenne pepper
½ teaspoon freshly ground black pepper
Vegetable oil for frying

Heat the butter in a frying pan over low heat. Add the onion and sauté for 3 minutes. Add the garlic, ginger, cumin, and cardamom; sauté the mixture, stirring occasionally, another 3–4 minutes, and reserve.

Mix together the meat, bread crumbs, egg, mint, chile, lemon juice, salt, cayenne, and black pepper.

Add the onion mixture to the meat mixture and shape into patties about 2 inches in diameter.

Heat about ¾ inch of oil in a deep frying pan over medium heat. Add the patties two or three at a time, to give the oil time to reheat, and cook until the patties are well browned, turning them frequently. Drain them on paper towels and serve with a mixed salad and warmed pita bread.

Cubed Beef
Gayki Boti

Preparation and cooking time: 45 minutes   *Serves 4*

- 3 pounds stewing beef, cubed
- 3 medium-size onions, peeled and chopped
- 4 garlic cloves, peeled and chopped
- ¼ cup lemon juice
- 2 teaspoon Dijon mustard
- 1 teaspoon salt
- ½ cup vegetable oil

Heat the oven to 400°F.

Combine all the ingredients with ½ cup water in a heavy casserole or ovenproof dish and bake for 40 minutes.

Serve with Raw Spinach Salad (page 181) and warmed pita bread.

Roast Ginger Beef
Bhuna Adrak-Walla Gosht

Preparation and cooking time: *Serves 4*
about 1 hour 20 minutes

- 3½ pounds boneless sirloin roast
- 4 tablespoons chopped parsley
- 2 inch piece of fresh ginger root, peeled and grated
- 2 green chiles, seeded (optional) and chopped
- 2 tablespoons Dijon mustard
- 2 tablespoons lemon juice
- ¼ teaspoon salt

Heat the oven to 300°F. Place the beef in a greased baking pan, fat side up.

Combine the parsley, ginger, chiles, mustard, lemon juice, and salt in a food processor or blender. Rub the mixture all over the meat, covering it well. Bake about 1 hour 10 minutes for medium-rare meat, a little longer for medium. Serve with warmed pita bread and Lemon Lentils (page 198).

Spiced Kashmiri Lamb
Kashmiri Gosht

Preparation and cooking time: 1¼ hours   Serves 4

- 1 **pound boneless lean lamb, cut in large bite-size pieces**
- 2 **large onions, peeled and sliced**
- 1¾ **cups yoghurt, beaten**
- 3 **tablespoons vegetable oil**
- 1 **tablespoon poppy seeds**
- ½ **teaspoon salt**
- 5 **ounces slivered almonds**
- ¾ **tablespoon chili powder**
- ¼ **teaspoon powdered saffron**

Put the lamb, onions, yoghurt, and oil in a saucepan and mix well. Bring the mixture to a boil, lower the heat, and simmer gently, uncovered, until the meat is tender, about 45 minutes, adding a little hot water as necessary.

Grind the poppy seeds in a mortar, an electric coffee mill, or food processor or blender until they form a paste. Add the salt, poppy seed paste, and almonds to the saucepan, stirring them in well, and continue cooking until the mixture is dry.

Stir in the chili powder and saffron and let the mixture cook, almost frying, for 5 minutes. Serve hot with Basmati Pilaf (page 191).

Lamb and Cashew Stew
Kaju Gosht

Preparation and cooking time: 1¼–1½ hours　　　*Serves 5–6*

　½ cup vegetable oil
　2 pounds boneless lean lamb, cut in large bite-size pieces
　8 medium-size onions, peeled and finely chopped
　½ tablespoon salt
　8 cloves
　8 peppercorns
　3 cinnamon sticks
　1 tablespoon caraway seeds
　1 tablespoon cumin seeds
4–5 bay leaves
　1 cup plain yoghurt
8–10 garlic cloves, peeled and crushed
　3 tablespoons finely chopped coriander leaves

For the chile paste
10–15 green chiles, seeded
　¼ inch piece of fresh ginger root
　6 garlic cloves, peeled

For the cashew paste
　4 ounces cashews
　3 tablespoons sesame seeds
　3 tablespoons poppy seeds

Heat one-third the oil in a large saucepan over high heat. When hot, add the lamb and cook, stirring frequently, until it is browned on all sides, about 5 minutes.

Remove the lamb from the pan with a slotted spoon and reserve. Turn the heat to medium, add half the remaining oil and the onions, and cook, stirring frequently, until the onions soften, 7–8 minutes.

Return the lamb to the pan with the salt, spices, and hot water to cover. Bring to the boil, then simmer for 25 minutes, until the meat is cooked but not tender. Drain and reserve the water and return the mixture to the pan.

Meanwhile, make the chile paste by processing the chiles, ginger root, and garlic to a paste in a food processor, or in batches in a blender, and reserve. For the cashew paste, purée the nuts and seeds similarly and reserve.

Add the chile paste to the lamb and gently simmer the mixture over low heat for 10–15 minutes, adding a few table-spoonfuls of the reserved stock as necessary to prevent burning.

Add the cashew paste and simmer for another 10–15 minutes, adding stock as necessary.

Add the yoghurt and let it simmer for 5 minutes.

Add stock according to the thickness of sauce you desire. Simmer gently until the meat is tender, adding a little more stock as necessary.

Heat the rest of the oil in a small saucepan over medium-low heat and add the garlic. When the garlic is golden, add it to the stew with the chopped coriander, cover immediately, and cook gently for 5 more minutes. Uncover just before serving. Serve with Saffron Pilaf (page 189).

Minced Lamb Kebabs
Gosht Kabab

Preparation and cooking time: *Serves 6*
boiling the potatoes, plus 20–25 minutes

  2 pounds boneless lamb shoulder, cut in large dice
1½ inch piece of fresh ginger root, peeled and cut into
    3–4 pieces
  2 large potatoes, boiled, peeled, and chopped
  3 green chiles, seeded (optional) and chopped
 ½ cup plain yoghurt
 ½ teaspoon salt
  1 teaspoon black pepper

Heat the broiler. Place the lamb, ginger, potatoes, chiles, yoghurt, salt, and pepper in a food processor. Process for about 30 seconds (pulsing as it goes to keep the mixture moving properly) or until the mixture is a coarse purée.

Form the mixture into 6–8 patties, about 3 inches in diameter, and place them flat on a greased broiler pan.

Place the pan 4–5 inches under the heat source and cook the kebabs for 12–15 minutes, turning once, for medium, or longer if wished.

Serve the kebabs with pita bread and a fresh salad.

Note: You can also fry these kebabs in a lightly greased pan, though I prefer them broiled.

Roast Veal with Mustard and Ginger

Rai Adrak-Walla Bachra

Preparation and cooking time:
5 hours marinating, plus 3 hours 10 minutes

Serves 4–6

- 2 tablespoons vegetable oil
- 6 pounds loin of veal, boned and rolled
- 1 teaspoon cayenne pepper
- 2 tablespoons Dijon mustard (preferably flavored with green peppercorns)
- ½ cup lemon juice
- 1 teaspoon salt, plus extra for sprinkling
- 3 inch piece of fresh ginger root, peeled and grated
- 4 tablespoons finely chopped fresh parsley

Coat a roasting pan with the oil and place the veal in the pan.

Mix together the cayenne pepper, mustard, lemon juice, and salt, and rub this over the veal.

Top the mixture with the ginger, parsley, and a sprinkling of salt, and leave the meat to season in the refrigerator for 5 hours.

Heat the oven to 300°F. Bake the meat for 3 hours. Serve with Savory Onion Rice (page 190).

8
Vegetables

Nul Bazaar was only a few hundred steps from the house where I grew up in Bombay. With six sisters, visiting uncles, aunts, nephews, and nieces, there was always a great deal of shopping to be done. The bazaar was the center of great activity of all kinds, but the main one for us was buying food—everything from fresh vegetables and fruit to meat, fish, chicken, pulses, and spices.

My father and I would proceed from stall to stall and look for the very best quality at the best price. "You get what you pay for, sir," one vegetable vendor would respond to my father's comments. She was very prosperous looking, the weight of her gold earrings stretching her ear lobes, and had a bright red "bindi" in the center of her forehead. As she sprinkled water on her piles of vegetables to keep them crisp and fresh looking, she seemed always ready for a fight. But she enjoyed a laugh, too, and I looked forward to seeing her.

In the bazaar the day's produce was collected fresh from farmers and sold the same day. Selling began at 6:30 in the morning and by 11 A.M. all the fresh vegetables were gone. The fruit sellers' stalls would be open all day, but the shopkeepers would nap between 1 and 4 in the afternoon, covering their stalls with gunnysacks. After napping, they would roll up the gunnysacks and the marvelously colored fruit would reappear.

The bounty laid out before us in the bazaar was wonderful. We could touch the live poultry, smell the melons, squeeze the vegetables and fruit. In fact, we were encouraged to do so. It was an important part of shopping in the bazaar and taught me one of a cook's most important—and obvious—lessons: choose the freshest and most beautiful fruits and vegetables.

Alas, when I came to America as a young man I saw everything in the supermarkets wrapped in cellophane. Touching and smelling and examining too closely are frowned upon and discouraged, so participation by the shopper and the entire shopping experience is diminished. This is still true of most markets, I'm afraid, but there are some wonderful new markets for fruit and vegetables appearing in the West which are more in the style of the Orient. There is little cellophane or plastic in evidence, and one is free to touch, smell, and select the most appealing fruit and vegetables. We should all definitely patronize these markets.

Boiled Potatoes with Scallions and Chives

Aloo aur Hari Piyaz ki Sabzi

Preparation and cooking time: 10–15 minutes   *Serves 4*

1½ pounds small potatoes
6 tablespoons snipped chives
3 scallions, chopped
4 garlic cloves, peeled and chopped
4 tablespoons butter
2 sage leaves, chopped
½ green chile, seeded (optional) and chopped
Salt

Boil the potatoes in their jackets until they are just tender, then drain and cut each one into 2–3 pieces.

While the potatoes are still hot, add the chives, scallions, garlic, butter, sage, chile, and salt to taste. Serve hot.

Potatoes and Peas
Aloo Mattar

Preparation and cooking time: 30 minutes　　　　*Serves 6–8*

8 medium-size potatoes
½ cup vegetable oil
1 medium-size onion, peeled and sliced
2 teaspoons cumin seeds
1 teaspoon freshly ground black pepper
2 medium-size tomatoes, sliced
1 pound fresh shelled or frozen and defrosted green peas
　　Salt

Peel and slice the potatoes and reserve.

Heat the oil in a frying pan over medium-low heat. When hot, add the onion and cook until it begins to brown, stirring occasionally.

Add the potatoes and cook for 10 minutes over medium heat, stirring occasionally.

Add the cumin, pepper, tomatoes, peas, and salt to taste. Continue cooking, stirring occasionally, until the potatoes are crisp, 10–15 minutes.

Va-Va-Voom Potatoes
Khas Aloo

This dish is so good you'll be glad of any leftovers.

Preparation and cooking time: about 15 minutes   *Serves 6*

2½ **pounds small red potatoes**
 ½ **cup tarragon vinegar**
 ¼ **cup walnut oil**
 8 **dried red peppers, seeded (optional)**
 1 **teaspoon mustard seeds**
 1 **teaspoon salt**
1½ **teaspoons dill weed**

Boil the potatoes in their jackets. Do not overcook them; they should be just firm.

Combine the vinegar, oil, peppers, mustard seeds, salt, and dill weed in a saucepan.

Drain and halve the unskinned potatoes, mix them with the other ingredients and cook for 10 minutes, covered, over low heat. Serve hot.

Cucumber Raita
Kheera ka Raita

Preparation time: 5 minutes, plus chilling   *Serves 5–6*

1¾ cups plain yoghurt
 1 medium-size cucumber
 ½ teaspoon salt
 ½ teaspoon ground cumin
   Sprig of mint, chopped

Stir the yoghurt with a fork until it is smooth.

Grate the cucumber and stir it into the yoghurt with the salt, cumin, and mint. Chill slightly before serving.

Spicy Vegetarian Curry
Masaledar Sabzi

Preparation and cooking time: *Serves 4*
making the tamarind water, plus 35 minutes

 4 large potatoes, peeled and coarsely chopped
   Salt
 ¼ teaspoon turmeric
 3 medium-size tomatoes, blanched, skinned, and
   mashed
 ½ cup thick tamarind water (see note)
 2 tablespoons dark brown sugar

For the masala
 3 tablespoons vegetable oil

1 medium-size onion, peeled and finely chopped
1 inch piece of fresh ginger root
1–2 garlic cloves, peeled and pressed or finely chopped
2 teaspoons chili powder
2 tablespoons shredded coconut
1 teaspoon cumin seeds
1 tablespoon sesame seeds
1 tablespoon poppy seeds

First make the masala. Heat the oil in a saucepan over medium-low heat. When hot, add the onion and cook, stirring occasionally until it softens.

Add the rest of the masala ingredients to the pan and cook, stirring occasionally, for 3–4 minutes, until the mixture becomes reddish.

Add the potatoes and cook over medium heat, stirring frequently, for 3–4 minutes.

Add 3¾ cups hot water, salt, and the turmeric to the pan and simmer until the potatoes are just cooked.

Add the tomatoes, tamarind water, and sugar. Boil until the sugar dissolves. Serve with plain boiled rice.

Note: To make tamarind water, soak a small lump of tamarind in warm water for 15–20 minutes. Squeeze the tamarind with your fingers, then strain off the tamarind water.

Sautéed Mushrooms
Kumbhi Khas

Preparation and cooking time: 10 minutes   *Serves 4–6*

6 tablespoons butter
3 tablespoons lemon juice
½ teaspoon cayenne pepper
½ teaspoon cumin seeds
6 ounces button mushrooms, cleaned and sliced

Melt the butter in a frying pan over low heat and add the lemon juice, cayenne pepper, and cumin seeds. Cook for 3–4 minutes.

Add the mushrooms and sauté for 5–6 minutes.

Mushrooms Sautéed in Mustard Oil
Rai-Walli Kumbhi

Preparation and cooking time: about 5 minutes   *Serves 3–4*

3 tablespoons mustard oil
¼ cup lemon juice
4 bay leaves, crumbled
1 teaspoon chili powder
12 medium-size button mushrooms, sliced

Heat the oil in a saucepan over low heat. Add the lemon juice, bay leaves, and chili powder, and cook for 1 minute.

Add the mushrooms and cook for 3–4 minutes only. The mushrooms should not be overcooked.

Spicy Potatoes, Cauliflower, and Peas

Aloo Phoolgobi Mattar ki Sabzi

Preparation and cooking time: about 25 minutes   *Serves 6–8*

- ¼ cup vegetable oil
- 2 medium-size onions, peeled and chopped
- 2 large garlic cloves, peeled and chopped
- 2 green chiles, seeded (optional) and chopped
- ¼ teaspoon turmeric
- ½ teaspoon cayenne pepper
- 12 black peppercorns
- 6 medium-size potatoes
- 1 medium-size cauliflower, halved, cored, and cut into large florets
- ½ teaspoon salt
- ¼ cup lemon juice
- 1½ cups peas

Heat the oil in a large deep saucepan over low heat. When hot, add the onions, garlic, chiles, turmeric, cayenne pepper, and peppercorns. Cook the mixture 10 minutes, stirring occasionally.

Peel the potatoes and cut them into thick slices, then stir into the mixture. Stir in the cauliflower florets.

Add the salt, lemon juice, and 1 cup hot water. Continue cooking over low heat for about 25 minutes, adding the peas during the last 10 minutes of cooking.

Merchant's Spinach Purée
Palak Bharta

Preparation and cooking time: Serves 2
preparing the spinach, plus 10 minutes

1½ pounds fresh spinach, washed and trimmed, or 8
    ounces frozen spinach, defrosted
 2 scallions
 1 tablespoon butter
½ teaspoon salt
 1 tablespoon Dijon mustard

Add the spinach to a pan of boiling water and cook, stirring
occasionally, until it is tender, 1–3 minutes.

    Drain the spinach through a colander, pressing the greens
with the back of a spoon to get rid of excess moisture.

    Place the spinach, scallions, butter, salt, and mustard in a
food processor. Purée the mixture and serve hot.

Spinach Jannu

Palak Jannu

Preparation and cooking time:
preparing the spinach, plus 10 minutes

Serves 2–3

- 1½ pounds spinach, washed and trimmed, or 8 ounces frozen spinach, defrosted
- 1 medium-size onion, peeled and chopped
- 1–2 garlic cloves
  Juice of ½ lemon
- 1 tablespoon Dijon mustard
  Pinch of salt
- ¼ teaspoon freshly ground black pepper
- 4 tablespoons butter

Add the spinach to a pan of boiling water and cook, stirring occasionally, until it is tender, 1–3 minutes.

Drain the spinach through a colander, pressing the greens with the back of a spoon to get rid of excess moisture.

Place the spinach in a food processor or blender with the onion, garlic, lemon juice, mustard, salt, pepper, and butter. Purée the mixture and serve hot.

Stuffed Potato Patties
Aloo Tikki

Preparation and cooking time: *Serves 4*
boiling the potatoes, plus about 25 minutes

- 4 large potatoes, boiled in their jackets until very tender
- 1 tablespoon vegetable oil
- ¼ teaspoon salt
- 1 teaspoon cayenne pepper
- 2 tablespoons cream
- 3 large eggs
- 4 tablespoons butter

For the pea stuffing
- 8 ounces green peas, defrosted if frozen
- ½ fresh green chile, seeded (optional) and chopped
- 2 tablespoons chopped parsley

For the spinach stuffing
- ½ pound fresh spinach, washed and trimmed, or 3 ounces frozen spinach, defrosted
- 1–2 green chiles, seeded (optional) and chopped
  Pinch of salt
- ¼ teaspoon freshly ground black pepper

First make one of the stuffings. For the pea stuffing, cook the peas in boiling water until done and drain them through a colander. Stir in the chile and parsley.

For the spinach stuffing, cook the spinach in boiling water until done and drain it through a colander. Stir in the chiles, salt, and pepper.

To make the patties, peel the boiled potatoes, then mash them with the oil, salt, pepper, and cream.

With your hands, make round patties about 3 inches in diameter and ¼ inch thick. The potato mixture has to be well mashed to make fairly thin patties. A food processor does this job beautifully.

Place a portion of spinach or pea filling on one patty, place another patty over it, and pinch the edges together gently to seal them.

Beat the eggs together with a fork. Dip the patties into the beaten egg mixture. This helps hold them together and also gives them a nice crust.

Heat the butter in a large frying pan over medium-low heat. When hot, carefully add the patties, without overlapping them, and cook about 6 minutes, turning once, or until they are nicely browned. Serve right away.

Sautéed Zucchini
Tali Gilki

Preparation and cooking time: 10 minutes   *Serves 4*

3–4 medium-size zucchini
  2 tablespoons butter
  ¼ cup lemon juice
  4 sage leaves, chopped, or ½ teaspoon dried sage
  ¼ teaspoon freshly ground black pepper
  ¼ teaspoon salt

Cut the zucchini into ⅛-inch slices, discarding the very ends.

Melt the butter in a deep frying pan over medium-low heat. When hot, stir in the zucchini and the rest of the ingredients, and cook, stirring frequently, until the zucchini is barely tender. Serve immediately.

Potato Chaat
Aloo Chaat

Leftover boiled potatoes and beans are fine for this dish. *Chaat* in Hindi means "something that excites the palate."

Preparation and cooking time: *Serves 4*
boiling the potatoes and beans, plus about 10 minutes

- **4 tablespoons butter**
- **1 pound potatoes, boiled and sliced**
  Pinch of salt
- **1 tablespoon Dijon mustard**
- **¼ pound French beans, cooked**
- **1 tablespoon chopped parsley**

Melt the butter in a frying pan over medium-low heat. Add the potatoes, salt, mustard, and beans. Stir to combine.

Cook the mixture for about 10 minutes, until it is thoroughly hot. Sprinkle the parsley over it, and serve immediately.

Fried Vegetable Toast
Sabzi-Walli Toast

Preparation and cooking time: 50 minutes   *Serves 6–8*

  4 ounces carrots, chopped
  8 ounces green cabbage, chopped
  8 ounces shelled peas, defrosted if frozen
  3 large potatoes, peeled
  4 tablespoons cornstarch
  6 coriander leaves, chopped
      Juice of 2 lemons
8–10 green chiles, seeded (optional) and finely chopped
      Salt
 12 slices of white bread
      Vegetable oil for frying

Cook the carrots and cabbage in boiling salted water until they are almost tender. Add the peas and continue cooking until all are tender.

Drain, then mash the vegetables.

Meanwhile boil the potatoes until tender, then mash them.

Add the potatoes to the mashed vegetables with the cornstarch, coriander leaves, lemon juice, chiles, and salt to taste, mixing well. Mix in more cornstarch, if necessary, to make a fairly stiff paste.

Cut the bread slices into halves and spread a thick layer of vegetable mixture over them.

Heat about 1 inch of oil in a large frying pan over medium-low heat. When hot, fry the slices, a few at a time, with the mixture face down, for 4–5 minutes, until the vegetable mixture begins to brown.

Serve the vegetable toasts hot with Tomato Chutney (page 225).

Clove-Garlic Mixed Vegetables
Ganga Jumna Sabzi

The Ganga and the Jumna are two holy rivers in India that give their name to this quite heavenly mixture.

Preparation and cooking time: about 40 minutes   Serves 6

  6 medium-size carrots, peeled
  2 medium-size potatoes, peeled
  8 ounces shelled green peas, defrosted if frozen
  8 ounces green beans, topped and tailed, defrosted if frozen
  4 medium-size beets
  3 medium-size tomatoes
  ½ cup vegetable oil
  2 medium-size onions, peeled and chopped
  4 bay leaves, crumbled
 12 cloves
  6 garlic cloves
  ½ tablespoon chili powder

Chop and combine the carrots, potatoes, peas, beans, beets, and tomatoes in a bowl and reserve.

Heat the oil in a saucepan over medium-low heat and add the onions, bay leaves, and cloves. Cook them for 5–6 minutes, stirring occasionally.

Add the garlic and chili powder and continue cooking for 5–6 minutes.

Add the reserved vegetables and cook for 15 minutes, until vegetables are tender. Serve hot.

Cayenned Corn

Makai ke Dane Mirch-Walli

Preparation and cooking time: 15 minutes   *Serves 4*

4–5 ears corn
  3 tablespoons butter
  ½ cup light cream
  2 garlic cloves, peeled and chopped
    Pinch of salt
  ½ teaspoon cayenne pepper

Cut the raw corn kernels away from the cobs with a sharp knife.

Melt the butter in a frying pan over low heat. Add the corn, then the cream, garlic, salt, and cayenne.

Simmer gently for 8–10 minutes until the corn is tender. Serve right away.

Stewed Cauliflower and Tomatoes
Gobi Tamatar

Preparation and cooking time: 35–40 minutes   *Serves 4*

¼ cup vegetable oil
½ medium-size onion, peeled and chopped
3 bay leaves, crumbled
1 medium-size cauliflower, cleaned and cut into small florets
2 medium-size tomatoes, chopped
¼ cup vinegar
½ teaspoon salt
½ teaspoon cayenne pepper
  Juice of ½ lemon

Heat the oil in a saucepan over medium-low heat. Add the onion and cook until it begins to brown.

Add the bay leaves and cauliflower, then the tomatoes, vinegar, salt, cayenne, and lemon juice. Cover and cook for 30 minutes over low heat, until the cauliflower is tender.

Spicy Stewed Cauliflower and Potatoes

Masaledar Gobi Aloo

Preparation and cooking time: 45–50 minutes   *Serves 4–6*

¼ cup vegetable oil
1 medium-size onion, peeled and chopped
2 large potatoes, peeled and cut into small pieces
1 teaspoon cayenne pepper
¼ cup lemon juice
1 teaspoon salt
¼ teaspoon turmeric
1 medium-size cauliflower, washed and cut into florets
1 green chile, seeded (optional) and sliced
1 dried red chile, seeded (optional) and crushed
½ cup plain yoghurt mixed with ¼ cup water

Heat the oil in a large saucepan over medium-low heat. Add the onion and cook until it begins to turn brown, stirring occasionally.

Stir in the pieces of potatoes and cook until they also begin to brown, stirring frequently.

Add the cayenne pepper, lemon, salt, and turmeric; cook over medium-low heat for 2–3 minutes, stirring occasionally.

Add the cauliflower, green and red chiles, and the yoghurt-water mixture and stir well.

Continue cooking until the vegetables are tender, 20–30 minutes.

Richard's Cinnamon-Dill Carrots

Darchini aur Suwa-Walla Gajar

Preparation and cooking time: 20 minutes   *Serves 6*

  6 large carrots (1 per person)
  2 tablespoons butter
  ½ teaspoon ground cinnamon
  1 tablespoon honey
   Pinch of salt
  ½ teaspoon coarsely ground pepper
  ½ tablespoon chopped dill

Peel the carrots and cut them into 2-inch-long batons, uniformly slender.

Boil the carrots until tender but still firm, about 5 minutes.

Pour off the water. Add the butter to the pan and cook over very low heat for 2–3 minutes. Stir in the cinnamon, honey, salt, pepper, and dill and serve right away.

Spicy Red Cabbage

Masaledar Lal Karam Kalle

Preparation and cooking time: 35–45 minutes   *Serves 6–8*

¼ cup vegetable oil
2 medium size onions, peeled and chopped
1 tablespoon cumin seeds
1 tablespoon chili powder
3 garlic cloves, peeled and finely chopped
2½ pounds red cabbage, cored and sliced
1 teaspoon salt
¼ cup tarragon vinegar

Heat the oil in a saucepan over medium-low heat. When hot, add the onions and cook, stirring occasionally, until they turn golden-brown.

Stir in the cumin seeds, chili powder, and garlic and let the mixture cook over low heat for 10 minutes.

Add the cabbage and mix well. Add the salt, then add the vinegar, and cover. Cook for 20–30 minutes over low heat until the cabbage is very soft.

Sautéed Red Cabbage and Raisins
Kismishi Lal Karem Kalle

Preparation and cooking time: about 15 minutes   *Serves 4–6*

¼ cup vegetable oil
1 medium-size onion, peeled and chopped
1 pound red cabbage, cored and finely chopped
¼ teaspoon cumin seeds
6 cloves
½ teaspoon salt
¼ teaspoon chili powder
1 apple, cored and sliced with skin
¼ cup lemon juice
   About 12 raisins

Heat the oil in a small saucepan over medium-low heat. When hot, add the onion and cook until the onion begins to brown, stirring occasionally.

Add the rest of the ingredients to the pan and cook over low heat for 10 minutes, stirring occasionally, until the cabbage is tender.

Broccoli in Garlic-Lemon Butter
Nimbu aur Lasson-Walli Broccoli

Preparation and cooking time: about 10 minutes   *Serves 3–4*

1 pound broccoli
6 tablespoons butter
1 teaspoon chili powder
4 garlic cloves, peeled and chopped
  Juice of 2 medium-size lemons
1 teaspoon cumin seeds

Discard any thick, coarse ends, and steam or boil the broccoli for 8–10 minutes, until just tender. Be careful not to overcook so it remains green and slightly crisp.

Meanwhile, melt the butter in a saucepan with the rest of the ingredients over low heat.

Pour the garlic-lemon butter over the broccoli and serve.

Green Beans in Mustard Sauce

Frazbeen Sarsoon ke Tail-Walli

Preparation and cooking time: 20 minutes　　　　　*Serves 4–6*

- 1 pound green beans
- 1 tablespoon Dijon or Düsseldorf mustard
  Salt and freshly ground black pepper
- 1–1½ tablespoons lemon juice
- ¼ cup olive oil

Top and tail the beans, but leave them whole. Soak them in very cold water for 5–6 minutes.

Drain the beans and steam them in a vegetable steamer for about 5 minutes, until just tender. Alternatively, cook them in boiling water for 5 minutes. The important thing is not to overcook them.

Meanwhile, spoon the mustard into a small bowl and add the salt, pepper, and lemon juice. Stir to blend, then whisk in the oil.

Drain the beans. Add the mustard sauce to them, toss to coat well, and serve immediately.

Stewed Eggplant
Baygan ka Bharta

Preparation and cooking time: 25–30 minutes   *Serves 4*

¼ cup vegetable oil
1 medium-size onion, peeled and chopped
4 bay leaves, crumbled
1 large eggplant
½ teaspoon chili powder
½ teaspoon salt
1¾ cups canned tomatoes including juices
2 tablespoons red wine vinegar
½ teaspoon caraway seeds
¼ cup lemon juice

Heat the oil in a frying pan over medium-low heat, add the onion and bay leaves, and cook them for 4–5 minutes, stirring occasionally.

Meanwhile, peel the eggplant, slice it, then cut it into pieces. Add them and the rest of the ingredients to the pan.

Raise the heat until the mixture begins to simmer, then cover, reduce the heat, and simmer for 20 minutes, until the eggplant is very tender.

Fresh Asparagus
in Mustard Dressing

Sarsoon-Walli Asparagus

Preparation and cooking time: about 10 minutes   *Serves 4*

20 asparagus spears
 2 tablespoons Dijon mustard
 2 tablespoons tarragon vinegar
 ¼ teaspoon salt
 ¼ teaspoon cayenne pepper

Steam the asparagus until tender, about 10 minutes.

Meanwhile, whisk together the mustard, tarragon vinegar, salt, and cayenne pepper.

Drain the asparagus, if necessary, and place it on a warmed serving platter. Pour the mustard sauce over and serve.

Spiced Okra
Masala Bhindi

Preparation and cooking time: 20 minutes   *Serves 4–6*

1 tablespoon ground cumin
½ teaspoon turmeric
1 teaspoon chili powder
¼ teaspoon salt
¼ cup lemon juice
1 teaspoon Dijon mustard
½ pound okra (about 30 small pods)
¼ cup vegetable oil

Mix the cumin, turmeric, chili powder, salt, and lemon juice in a small bowl.

Add the mustard and mix to make a rather wet paste.

Cut the stems off the okra pods. Then split them three-quarters the way down. Split them again, dividing the pods into four equal parts that are held together by the narrow end tip.

Pour a little of the paste into the openings, and spread it lightly over all but the narrow tip. Sprinkle with salt.

Heat the oil in a small frying pan over low heat and fry the pods, covered, until they are tender, about 10 minutes, turning them once.

Fasting Day Potatoes
Aftari Aloo

This is a celebratory dish I created after a day of fasting.

Preparation and cooking time: about 20 minutes   *Serves 3–4*

 4 medium-size potatoes
 3 tablespoons vegetable oil
 1 medium-size onion, peeled and diced
12 black peppercorns
½ teaspoon cumin seeds
 3 garlic cloves, peeled and chopped
   Pinch of salt
¼ cup lemon juice
 1 bunch fresh dill, stems discarded and chopped

Peel and slice the potatoes.

Heat the oil in a frying pan over medium-low heat. When hot, add the onion and cook until it begins to brown, stirring occasionally.

Add the potatoes and remaining ingredients. Cook for about 15 minutes, stirring occasionally, until the potatoes are tender. Serve hot.

Grilled Zucchini with Cumin Butter

Zeera Mukhon-Walli Gilki

Preparation and cooking time: 10 minutes   *Serves 6*

6 medium-size zucchini

For the cumin butter
½ tablespoon chili powder
3 tablespoons butter
¼ teaspoon salt
4–6 garlic cloves
1 teaspoon cumin seeds, bruised in a mortar

Heat the broiler. Stir the cumin butter ingredients together in a bowl.

Slice the zucchini into halves lengthwise and spread the butter over them.

Place them on a broiler rack about 5 inches from the source of heat. Cook for 8 minutes, until just tender.

Coconut Dumplings and Vegetable Stew

Dhokle

This is one of the great Indian dishes.

Preparation and cooking time: *Serves 6*
*12 hours soaking the chick-peas, plus preparing the coconut, then
1½ hours*

> 4 ounces yellow chick-peas (kabli chana), picked over and washed
> 4 ounces brown chick-peas (kala chana), picked over and washed
> 1 cup vegetable oil
> 1 medium-size onion, peeled and chopped
> 6 bay leaves, crumbled
> ¼ pound cauliflower, cut into small florets
> ¼ pound French beans, topped and tailed
> ¼ pound green peas
> ¼ pound butter beans, topped and tailed
> 1 green or red pepper
> ½ pound tomatoes
> ½ pound chick-pea (gram) flour
> ½ pound millet flour
> ¼ pound rice flour
> 3 tablespoons vegetable oil
> 2 tablespoons clarified butter
> 2 teaspoons ground coriander
> ½ teaspoon turmeric
>   About 1 teaspoon chili powder
>   Meat of ½ large coconut (page 85), grated
>   Salt
> ½ pound potatoes, cut in large dice
> ¼ pound eggplant, cut in large dice

For the green spice paste
6–8 green chiles, seeded (optional)
  2 whole garlic bulbs, peeled and chopped
  1 inch piece of fresh ginger root, grated
  1 tablespoon cumin seeds

Cover the yellow and brown chick-peas with plenty of cold water to cover and leave them to soak for 12 hours. Drain well.

Pound the ingredients for the green spice paste in a mortar, or purée them in a food processor or in batches in a blender, and reserve.

Heat the oil in a large saucepan. When hot, add the onion and bay leaves and cook over medium-low heat, stirring occasionally, until the onion is light brown.

Add the cauliflower, French beans, peas, drained chick-peas, butter beans, and pepper to the onion. Cook for 15 minutes, stirring occasionally, then add three-quarters of the green spice paste, stirring.

Chop the tomatoes, stir them into the saucepan, and cook for 5 minutes.

Add 5 cups hot water to the pan and continue cooking.

Meanwhile, mix the three flours in a soup plate and add the oil and clarified butter. Add the remaining green spice paste, the coriander, turmeric, chili powder, and three-quarters of the grated coconut and stir to taste. Reserve the remaining grated coconut. (Keep the rest of the coconut meat for another dish.)

Stir the flour mixture to make a medium firm dough, adding a little water if necessary.

Form the dough into long, flat, fist-shaped dumplings. When the vegetable mixture begins to boil, add the dumplings, potatoes, the rest of the grated coconut, and the eggplant. Simmer the mixture over low heat for 30–40 minutes. Serve with plain boiled rice.

9
Salads

I include several of my favorite salads here. There is no "cooking" as such in them, unless you actually boil the beets, as salads are best slightly chilled and crisp. Then they are cool and refreshing. This means that all the ingredients should be washed and carefully dried: water makes a salad soggy.

One of the very best salads is simply a great lettuce, properly washed and dried, then chilled, and dressed with a superior olive oil, a little salt, and fresh lemon juice. It never fails. Don't forget to toss it, or any mixed or dressed salad, thoroughly. Most people stint on the tossing. Tossing is part of the ritual of salad making and should not be neglected under any circumstances.

If you're fortunate enough to have your own garden, even a small one, you will be immensely rewarded. There is absolutely nothing like salad ingredients taken straight from the garden to the salad bowl. I have had a garden for years, which I tend with my friend Dick Robbins in a rather haphazard way because of our busy schedules. But it rewards me, despite neglect.

Green Lentil Salad

Haridal ka Salaad

This original salad is made with leftovers from my Moong Dal (page 202) recipe, and it is very good indeed.

Preparation time: *Serves 4–6*
making and chilling the Moong Dal, plus 10 minutes

> 1 medium-size onion, peeled and chopped
> 1 green chile, seeded (optional) and chopped
> 1 small bunch of parsley or watercress, stems removed
> Juice of 1 lemon
> 1–1¼ pounds leftover cold Moong Dal (page 202)

Mix the onion, chopped chile, parsley or watercress leaves, and lemon juice together.

Stir the mixture into the dal and serve cold.

Watercress, Celeriac, and Chicory Salad

Hare Patton ka Salaad

Preparation time: about 10 minutes   *Serves 4–6*

3 bunches of watercress, stems removed
1 small celeriac, peeled and cut in thin juliene strips
2 heads of endive, divided into leaves

For the dressing
1 tablespoon chopped parsley
1 tablespoon finely chopped onion
1 tablespoon finely chopped cornichons
1 tablespoon chopped capers
½ teaspoon finely chopped garlic
½ teaspoon Dijon mustard
1 teaspoon lemon juice
1½ teaspoons red wine vinegar
2 tablespoons olive oil
Salt and freshly ground black pepper

Prepare the vegetables and combine them in a salad bowl.

Mix together the parsley, onion, cornichons, capers, and garlic with the mustard, lemon juice, and vinegar. Add the oil, season to taste, and mix well.

Pour the dressing over the vegetables and toss well just before serving.

Tomato and Onion Salad

Tamatar aur Piyaz ka Salaad

Preparation time: 5 minutes   *Serves 4–6*

3 large tomatoes, cut into wedges
1 medium-size onion, peeled and very thinly sliced
1 tablespoon chopped fresh basil (optional)
1 tablespoon wine vinegar
1 tablespoon vegetable oil
½ teaspoon freshly ground black pepper
   Salt

Mix the tomatoes and onion slices in a salad bowl.

Combine the rest of the ingredients and toss them with the tomato and onion mixture.

Note: The tomato and onion mixture is also delicious with a mixture of plain yoghurt, salt, and pepper.

Mushrooms with Walnut Dressing

Kumbhi Akhroot ka Salaad

Preparation time: 10 minutes   *Serves 4*

2 tablespoons Dijon mustard
1 tablespoon tarragon vinegar
2 tablespoons walnut oil
½ pound button mushrooms, wiped clean
2 tablespoons chopped parsley

Combine the mustard, vinegar, and walnut oil.

Slice the mushrooms thin, pour the mustard mixture over them, and toss well. Sprinkle the parsley over the top and serve.

Tuna Salad I

Tuna Machli ka Pahela Salaad I

Preparation time: 10 minutes   *Serves 4*

14 ounces canned tuna, drained well and flaked
2 tablespoons mayonnaise
1 tablespoon Dijon mustard
2 scallions, chopped, or ½ small onion, chopped
4–5 medium-size mushrooms, sliced
¼ teaspoon freshly ground black pepper
1 fresh green chile, seeded (optional) and chopped

Combine the tuna, mayonnaise, mustard, scallions, mushrooms, pepper, and chile.
Serve on open slices of rye or pumpernickel bread.

Tuna Salad II

Tuna Machli ka Doosra Salaad II

Preparation time: 10 minutes   *Serves 4*

14 ounces canned tuna, drained well and flaked
1 tablespoon chopped parsley
¼ teaspoon cayenne pepper
2 tablespoons mayonnaise
1 tablespoon Dijon mustard
1 medium-size onion, peeled and chopped

Combine the tuna, parsley, cayenne pepper, mayonnaise, mustard, and onion.

Serve on open slices of rye or pumpernickel bread.

Tuna Divina

Tuna Machli ka Teesra Salaad

This is what one has for lunch while arguing over what to have for dinner.

Preparation time: 10 minutes *Serves 4*

14 ounces canned tuna, drained well and flaked
 1 green or red pepper, chopped
12 capers
 1 teaspoon coarsely chopped dried red chiles, seeded (optional)
 2 teaspoons chopped parsley
   Juice of 1½ lemons
 2 tablespoons Dijon mustard
 2 tablespoons olive oil
 2 hard-boiled eggs, shelled and chopped
 1 medium-size onion, peeled and chopped
 2 tablespoons mayonnaise

Combine the tuna, pepper, capers, chopped dried chiles, parsley, lemon juice, mustard, oil, eggs, onion, and mayonnaise.

Serve on open slices of rye, pumpernickel, or other interesting bread.

Pistachio Raita

Piston-Walla Raita

This is more an accompaniment to spicy Indian dishes than a salad, but it is a good one as it cools the palate.

Preparation time. 5 minutes, plus chilling   Serves 6

3¼ cups plain yoghurt
  4 tablespoons rose water
  2 tablespoons clear honey
  3 dozen shelled chopped unsalted pistachios
     Pinch of ground saffron (optional)

Stir the yoghurt, rose water, honey, and pistachios together and chill the mixture.

    Sprinkle with the saffron, if wished, and serve.

Beets Vinaigrette
Seerke-Walli Saljam

Preparation time: 5 minutes   *Serves 4*

2 tablespoons oil
2 tablespoons tarragon vinegar
   Pinch of salt
   Pinch of cayenne pepper
1 tablespoon chopped parsley
6 medium-size beets, boiled, peeled, and sliced

Stir together the oil, vinegar, salt, cayenne pepper, and parsley. Pour the mixture over the beets and serve.

Tarragon-Walnut Potato Salad
Sukhi Pati Akhroot aur Aloo ka Salaad

Preparation and cooking time: 15–20 minutes   *Serves 4–6*

5 pounds small, preferably red potatoes
1 cup mayonnaise
¼ cup walnut oil
2 tablespoons tarragon vinegar
½ cup Dijon mustard
4 or more large sprigs of fresh dill, chopped
½ teaspoon salt
¼ teaspoon cayenne pepper
2 medium-size onions, peeled and chopped

Boil the potatoes in their skins until they are just tender.

Meanwhile, mix together the rest of the ingredients and reserve.

Refresh the potatoes under cold running water for 2–3 minutes only, drain well, and cut them in half.

Combine the mayonnaise mixture and the potatoes and refrigerate, covered, until ready to serve.

Caraway-Onion Potato Salad

Shazeera-Walla Piyaz aur Aloo ka Salaad

Preparation and cooking time: 15–20 minutes　　　*Serves 4–6*

5 pounds small potatoes
1 large onion, peeled and diced
4 garlic cloves, peeled and chopped
4 tablespoons caraway seeds
4 tablespoons chopped parsley
　Juice of 2 lemons
¼ cup Dijon mustard
¼ cup vegetable oil
5 dried red peppers, seeded (optional) and coarsely
　chopped
½ teaspoon salt

Boil the potatoes in their skins until they are just tender.

Meanwhile, mix together the rest of the ingredients and reserve.

Refresh the potatoes under cold running water for 2–3 minutes only, drain well, and cut them in halves.

Stir the onion mixture with the potatoes and refrigerate, covered, until ready to serve.

Chicory-Walnut Salad

Safaid Patte Akhroot ka Salaad

Preparation time: 5 minutes   *Serves 2*

3–4 heads of endive
  2 tablespoons walnut oil
  2 tablespoons tarragon vinegar
   Pinch of salt
   Handful of chopped walnuts

Cut the heads of chicory across into bite-size slices and put them in a salad bowl.

Mix the rest of the ingredients together, toss them into the chicory, and serve.

Note: 1–2 garlic cloves, peeled and pressed, are an excellent addition to the dressing as the flavor of garlic is delicious with walnuts.

Chile-Tomato Salad

Mirch aur Tamatar ka Salaad

Preparation time: 5 minutes, plus chilling   *Serves 2*

  12 cherry tomatoes or 6 small tomatoes
  ½ bunch of parsley, stems removed and chopped
  ½ hot green chile, seeded (optional) and chopped
   1 teaspoon Dijon mustard
1½ teaspoons vegetable oil
   2 tablespoons lemon juice
    Pinch of salt
    Pinch of cayenne pepper

Halve the cherry tomatoes or quarter the small tomatoes.

Mix the chopped parsley and chile with the tomatoes and chill.

Combine the mustard, vegetable oil, lemon juice, salt, and cayenne pepper for the dressing and reserve.

Add the dressing to the chilled tomatoes just before serving.

Dressed Green Salad

Hara Salaad

Preparation time: 10 minutes   *Serves 2–4*

1–2 **heads of salad greens**
  2 **tablespoons olive oil**
    Juice of ½ lemon
 ¼ **teaspoon coarsely ground black pepper**
    Salt

Wash and pat the salad greens dry with paper towels or a tea towel just before making the salad.

Mix together the rest of the ingredients, toss them well into the leaves, and serve immediately.

Tomato Mint Raita
Phoodina Raita

Preparation time: 5–10 minutes   *Serves 4*

   2 medium-size onions, cut in half, then thinly sliced
   2 medium-size tomatoes, peeled and thinly sliced
   1 cup plain yoghurt
3–4 fresh mint sprigs, leaves removed and chopped
   1 2-inch green chile, seeded (optional) and finely
     chopped
   ¾ teaspoon ground cumin (or ½ teaspoon chili
     powder, if you prefer it a bit spicier)
   ¼ teaspoon salt

Combine the onions and tomatoes with the yoghurt.

Add the mint, chile, cumin or chili powder, and salt. Mix well and serve.

Raw Spinach Salad
Palak Salaad

Preparation time: 5–10 minutes   *Serves 4*

- 3 tablespoons olive oil
- 2 tablespoons tarragon vinegar
- 2 tablespoons capers, chopped
- 1½ teaspoons salt
- 1 pound spinach, freshly washed, stems removed and dried
- 1 large onion, preferably red, peeled and thinly sliced

Make the dressing by combining the oil, vinegar, capers, and salt. Just before serving, pour the dressing over the spinach and sliced onion. Toss thoroughly and serve.

Note: Another very good dressing for this simple salad is made by combining 2 tablespoons prepared spicy mustard, juice of 1 large lemon, and 3 tablespoons olive oil.

10

Rice

I never minded inviting friends over to taste my experimental dinners when cooking. Even though I am now more certain of my repertoire, I still enjoy experimenting and still like to whip up something that just "happens," depending on my mood, my ingredients, and the time I have to cook a meal. After running around all day on appointments, I sometimes have fifteen minutes to cook a meal. Often guests will be arriving soon and I must come up with a meal. But whether you have half a day or fifteen minutes to cook, meals should be prepared with gusto and feeling. This is one of the true enjoyments of cooking, and no doubt I really begin to relax for the first time at the end of the day in my kitchen.

Cooking rice causes great anxiety with some people. This is really unnecessary if, first of all, you tell yourself to *stop worrying*. Do *observe* what you do as you prepare a rice dish. Notice the appearance of the ingredients as you add them—don't just toss in the required amounts. Remember what you are doing. As you gain experience, you will learn to judge the correct proportions by sight. Then you will be able to judge for yourself whether you have added the right amounts, and using scales and a measuring cup will become less and less critical.

In my recipes I have given specific amounts of water for the rice used. To be honest with you, my rule of thumb when cooking rice is to fill the pan with water ½ inch above the level of the prepared rice.

If you make a mistake, my feeling is not to bother with great apologies to your guests. This embarrasses most people. Accept the mistake with good grace and learn from it.

There are different kinds of rice available, but before you buy them in bulk, buy smaller quantities of various sorts and try them all until you find the ones you like best. But never, never buy "instant" rice. It is absolutely dreadful. I do use standard packaged long-grain rice, which is available in every supermarket, but I prefer basmati rice, found in almost all Indian food shops.

Basmati is a special long-grain rice from India and Pakistan that has a unique flavor and aroma. It must be picked over as it sometimes contains small stones and twigs, and washed in several changes of water. This rinses off the excess starch, which causes grains of rice to stick together. Basmati rice is then always soaked in more fresh water for thirty minutes or so and drained, which cuts down on the amount of water used in cooking. The result is worth every instant of extra bother.

Cardamom and Coriander Rice

Kotmir Illaichi-Wale Chaaval

Preparation and cooking time: about 45 minutes   *Serves 6–8*

  2 tablespoons butter
2¼ cups long-grain rice
  4 black cardamom pods
  ½ teaspoon cayenne pepper
  ½ teaspoon salt
  3 tablespoons finely chopped fresh coriander leaves or
     parsley

Melt the butter in a saucepan over medium-low heat. Add the rice, cardamom pods, and cayenne pepper; cook for 6–7 minutes, stirring constantly. Watch carefully so the rice does not stick or burn.

Stir in 3¼ cups water and the salt. Bring the water to the boil, then cover the pan tightly and cook over very low heat for about 20 minutes, or until the grains are just tender.

Remove the pan from the heat and let the rice rest, covered, for 5–10 minutes.

Sprinkle the chopped coriander or parsley over the rice and serve.

Green Pea Pilaf
Mattar Pullao

Preparation and cooking time: about 45 minutes   *Serves 8–10*

    1 cup vegetable oil
    3 medium-size onions, peeled and chopped
    2 cinnamon sticks, broken up
    1 inch piece of fresh ginger root, chopped
    1 teaspoon chili powder
    ¼ teaspoon turmeric
    1 teaspoon cumin seeds
 3½ cups long-grain rice
    1 pound shelled peas, defrosted if frozen
    4 tablespoons butter

Heat the oil in a large saucepan over medium-low heat. When hot, add 2 of the chopped onions, cinnamon sticks, ginger, chili powder, turmeric, and cumin seeds and cook for 10 minutes.

Carefully add 5 cups water and bring to the boil. Add the rice, lower the heat, and simmer for 15 minutes, until the rice is fluffy.

Add the peas, stir well, and cook 10 minutes longer.

Meanwhile, melt the butter in a pan over medium heat, add the remaining chopped onion, and cook, stirring frequently, until the onion browns and crisps.

Spread the hot onion and butter over the top of the pilaf to serve.

Kichri Rice
Kichri Chaaval

Preparation and cooking time: about 1 hour   *Serves 6*

 2 tablespoons butter
 1 medium-size onion, peeled and chopped
12 cloves
 1 cinnamon stick, broken up
 ¼ teaspoon ground cumin
 5 black cardamom pods
 ¼ teaspoon ground turmeric
 ½ cup toor dal (see page 197), picked over, washed, and
    drained well
1¾ cups long-grain rice
 2 garlic cloves, peeled and chopped

Melt the butter in a large saucepan over medium-low heat.
Add the onion and cook, stirring occasionally, until it begins
to brown.

Stir in the cloves, cinnamon, cumin, cardamom, and turmeric and cook for 1–2 minutes.

Add the drained dal and continue to cook for another 3–4
minutes, stirring occasionally.

Add 2½ cups water and bring it to a boil.

Add the rice and garlic, cover tightly, reduce the heat, and
simmer gently for 40–45 minutes.

Chopped Meat Pilaf
Qeema Pullao

Preparation and cooking time: about 45 minutes   *Serves 8–10*

½ cup vegetable oil
2 medium-size onions, peeled and chopped
2 cinnamon sticks, broken up
1 inch piece of fresh ginger root, chopped
1 teaspoon chili powder
¼ teaspoon turmeric
1 pound chopped beef or lamb
5 cups long-grain rice
¼ cup plain yoghurt
4 hard-boiled eggs

Heat the oil in a large saucepan over medium-low heat. When hot, add the onions, cinnamon, ginger, chili powder, and turmeric and cook until the onions brown, stirring occasionally.

Add the meat to the pan and cook, stirring frequently, for 10 minutes.

Add 2½ cups water to the pan and bring to a boil. Stir the rice in well, add the yoghurt, turn the heat to low, and cook, stirring occasionally, for 15 minutes, until the rice is tender.

Shell and quarter the eggs and place them around the pilaf to serve.

Saffron Pilaf
Zafrani Pullao

I invited Vanessa Redgrave to dinner and hoped that she would agree to play Olive Chancellor in *The Bostonians*. She loved the Saffron Pilaf, the Green Lentil Dal (page 200), the Baked Stuffed Carp (page 62), and the Tomato Mint Raita (page 180), but said "no" to *The Bostonians*. The delights of this menu were slow to act, but effective in the end. Two years later she said "yes."

Preparation and cooking time: about 35 minutes　　　*Serves 3–4*

　2 tablespoons butter
　1 cinnamon stick
1¼ cups chicken stock
　½ teaspoon salt
　4 bay leaves, crumbled
　2 cups rice
　8 strands of saffron
　5 ounces slivered almonds

Melt the butter in a large saucepan with the cinnamon stick. Add 1¾ cups water, the stock, salt, and bay leaves and bring the liquid to a boil.

Add the rice, cover, and cook over very low heat for 10 minutes.

Add the saffron and cook for another 10 minutes, stirring occasionally, until the rice is tender.

Sprinkle with the almonds and serve.

Savory Onion Rice

Bhuni Piyaz ke Chaaval

Preparation and cooking time: about 40 minutes   *Serves 8*

   2 tablespoons butter
   1 medium-size onion, peeled and chopped
   4 black cardamom pods
1¾ cups chicken stock
   2 cups long-grain rice

Melt the butter in a large saucepan over medium-low heat. Add the onion and cook, stirring occasionally, until the onion begins to brown.

Stir in the cardamom pods, then add the stock and 1¼ cups water. Bring the liquid to a boil.

Add the rice, cover tightly, and turn the heat to very low. Cook for 20 minutes, stirring occasionally, until the rice is tender.

Basmati Pilaf
Basmati Pullao

Preparation and cooking time:
1 hour soaking and draining, plus 40 minutes

Serves 4

1 cup basmati rice, picked over
2 tablespoons vegetable oil
1 medium-size onion, peeled and chopped
2 inch piece of cinnamon stick
2 cloves
1 bay leaf, crumbled
½ cup cashew nuts
¼ cup seedless raisins
1 level teaspoon salt

Wash the rice in several changes of cold water until the water is clear, then cover it with plenty more cold water and leave it to soak for 30 minutes.

Let the rice drain through a sieve for about 30 minutes.

Heat the vegetable oil in a large frying pan over medium-low heat and lightly cook the onion until it is soft.

Add the drained rice, cinnamon, cloves, bay leaf, cashew nuts, and sultanas and stir-fry the mixture for 2 minutes over medium heat.

Add 2½ cups water to the pan with the salt. Cover tightly, turn the heat to low, and simmer for 20 minutes, adding a little extra water during cooking if necessary, until the rice is tender and fluffy and all the water is absorbed.

Yellow Turmeric Rice

Peela Chaaval

Preparation and cooking time: about 45 minutes   *Serves 8*

- 2 tablespoons butter
- 1 medium-size onion, peeled and chopped
- 4 black cardamom pods
- 2½ cups chicken stock
- 2 teaspoons cumin seeds
- ¼ teaspoon turmeric
- 2 cups long-grain rice

Melt the butter in a large saucepan over medium-low heat. Add the onion and cook, stirring occasionally, until the onion begins to brown.

Add the cardamom and cook for 1–2 minutes, stirring occasionally.

Add the stock and 1 cup water. Bring to a boil, then add the cumin seeds, turmeric, and rice.

Cook over low heat for 20 minutes, stirring occasionally, until the rice is tender.

Brown Rice with Bay Leaves

Tej Pati Chaaval

Brown rice is natural rice before it has been stripped of its outer layers, which are high in nutrients.

Preparation and cooking time: about 1 hour   *Serves 4–6*

    4 tablespoons butter
3–4 bay leaves, crumbled
    1 teaspoon salt
1¾ cups brown rice

Melt the butter in a large saucepan over low heat with the bay leaves.

Add 3¼ cups water and the salt to the pan and bring the liquid to the boil.

Add the rice, cover tightly, and turn the heat to low. Cook for 45 minutes, until the rice is just tender.

Cashew Rice

Kaju Chaaval

Preparation and cooking time: about 40 minutes   *Serves 4–6*

1¾ cups chicken stock
  2 dried red chiles, seeded (optional)
  1 cinnamon stick, broken up
 ¼ teaspoon salt
  1 teaspoon butter
2¼ cups long-grain rice
  5 ounces shelled raw cashews

Add the stock and 1¼ cups water to a large saucepan with the chiles, cinnamon stick, salt, and butter. Bring the liquid to a boil.

Stir in the rice and cashews, cover tightly, and cook over medium heat for 25 minutes, until the rice is tender.

11
Pulses

*F*ood helps us establish or ce-
ment relationships with other people, and this is the aspect of
cooking I find most enjoyable. You can do without many
things in life, but not food and the enjoyment of eating—
unless, of course, you become an ascetic or a fakir and become
radically self-sufficient. I could never become a hermit because
of missing the deep feeling of accomplishment and commu-
nion I have when preparing a meal for friends.

The recipes in this section are made with pulses (dried
lentils, beans, and peas) which nearly every culture uses in its
cooking and which appear at nearly every Indian meal. There
are many different varieties, and it is fun discovering the
different sorts available from Indian shops. They all have their
own particular qualities, which you will learn about as you
experiment with them. However, there are some general
guidelines.

All pulses should be picked over carefully to remove any
small stones, papery husks, and stems, then washed and
drained. Except for the familiar whole green European lentils,
most of the whole pulses need overnight soaking covered by

about three times their volume of cold water. Because whole Indian pulses are generally smaller than the ones used in the West, most of them need only two hours' soaking before they are ready to cook. If they have been hulled and/or split as with masoor dal, you can dispense with presoaking altogether. The exception, and naturally there is one, is with kabli and kala chana. Like their Western counterparts, these chick-peas need up to twelve hours' presoaking.

This being said, to avoid indigestion be sure to cook the prepared pulses in fresh water until they are tender. Undercooked pulses are bad news.

Some of the most common kinds of pulses used in Indian cooking are as follows:

Chana dal (or gram dal) are hulled and split chick-peas. Deep yellow in color, these pulses do not need soaking before cooking.

Kabli chana are yellow chick-peas. Unhulled and beige in color, they need overnight soaking before cooking.

Kala chana are small brown or black chick-peas. Like kabli chana, they require long presoaking and cooking to become tender.

Continental masoor are whole greenish-brown lentils. Flat and oval-shaped, they originated in the West and were adopted by India, so they should already be fairly familiar to you. They do not need presoaking.

Masoor are brown Indian lentils. Whole but smaller than continental masoor, they do not require presoaking.

Masoor dal are split masoor which are tiny and salmon-pink because they have also been hulled. They do not need presoaking and turn yellow when they cook.

Moong beans (or *hari dal*) are dark green, small, and slightly cylindrical in shape. They need 2–4 hours' soaking before cooking, but if oversoaked they will sprout and become moong bean sprouts so familiar in the West.

Moong dal chilka are split moong beans, green on one side and pale on the other. They do not need presoaking.

Moong dal are split, light yellow, and rectangular in shape because they are hulled. They do not need to be soaked before cooking.

Toor dal (or *arhar dal*) are a hulled, split pulse, a little larger than chana dal. Dull and yellow-colored, they do need presoaking.

Urid (or *black matpe*) are small, dull, and black, similar in size and shape to moong beans. They must be presoaked.

Urid dal are split urid that do not need to be soaked before cooking.

Washed *urid dal* are off-white because they have been hulled and washed as well as split. They do not require pre-soaking.

This list may seem long and overwhelming, but I suggest that you begin your experience in dal cooking with only one or two types of pulses first. Stick to the same type until you are familiar and quite confident with it. Then add another to your repertoire and so on. I would suggest you start with continental masoor, which is the most common kind, or possibly chana dal or masoor dal.

Lemon Lentils

Nimbu Masoor Dal

One of my favorite recipes, this one appeared in *The New York Times Magazine,* March 7, 1979. It's also a favorite of many people I've cooked for and has become a staple of my repertoire. I don't recall how it first happened. Probably by finding in the refrigerator a lemon that I flung into a pot of cooking dal in a pretty carefree way, but I always associate it with the actress Felicity Kendal, for whom I first made it.

I regard Felicity as my first pupil. She had come to England right after *Shakespeare-Wallah,* in which she starred, to make a life for herself, rather as the young girl, Lizzie, did in that film. She found a flat in Swan Court, Chelsea, with a tiny kitchen, and I gave her her first lesson in Indian cooking. Our menu was simple: tandoori chicken, pea pilaf, raita, and lemon dal. Felicity helped me peel onions and cut up ginger and tried not to get in my way too much. She watched very carefully as she must have watched her English relatives and friends, because in a very short time she was turning out delicious and quite complicated meals in that tiny kitchen, both Indian-style and traditional English ones. She is a natural-born cook, just as she is a natural-born actress; perhaps it is because one needs a sense of innate timing to be successful in both endeavors, cooking and acting.

Preparation and cooking time: about 1½ hours　　　*Serves 10–12*

1¼ **cups vegetable oil**
　2 **medium-size onions, halved and thinly sliced**
　4 **pieces of cinnamon stick, each about 2 inches long**
　2 **pounds masoor dal, picked over and washed**
　1 **tablespoon chopped fresh ginger root**
　5 **cups chicken stock**
　　Salt

1 teaspoon cayenne pepper
Juice of 1 lemon, plus the squeezed, seeded skin and
pulp
1 small onion, peeled and chopped
1 garlic clove, peeled and finely chopped
1 hot green chile, chopped, with seeds
4 bay leaves, crumbled
2 tablespoons chopped fresh coriander leaves

Heat ¾ cup of the oil in a large, deep saucepan over medium-low heat. When hot, add the sliced onions and cook, stirring, until they soften.

Add the cinnamon, lentils, and ginger to the pan and cook, stirring often, about 10 minutes.

Add the stock and 5 cups hot water, salt to taste, and cayenne pepper. Bring to the boil, then simmer about 10 minutes.

Add the lemon juice and squeezed shell and cook about 50 minutes longer, stirring often.

Heat the remaining ½ cup oil in a small pan and add the chopped onion, garlic, chile, and bay leaves. Cook, stirring, until the onion is browned.

Add this mixture, including the oil, to the lentils. Sprinkle with the chopped coriander leaves and serve hot.

Green Lentil Dal

Hara Masoor ki Dal

Preparation and cooking time: *Serves 4–6*
about 1½ hours

  2 tablespoons vegetable oil
  1 medium-size onion, peeled and chopped
12 cloves
  ½ cinnamon stick, broken
  1 pound continental masoor, picked over
1¾ cups canned beef broth
1½ teaspoons salt
1½ medium-size lemons
  ½ teaspoon chili powder

Heat the oil in a saucepan over medium-low heat. When hot, add the onion and cook, stirring occasionally, until it begins to brown. Stir in the cloves and broken cinnamon stick and cook for 1 minute.

Add the masoor and let cook for 5 minutes, stirring occasionally.

Add the consommé, 3¾ cups hot water, and the salt. Stir the mixture well, cover, and let it cook for 15 minutes.

After 15 more minutes over medium heat (it will be boiling), add the lemon juice, then toss in the rinds and add the chili powder. Cook, covered, for another 50 minutes, until the lentils are tender.

Chick-Pea Dal

Kabuli Chana

Preparation and cooking time: *Serves 6–8*
soaking the pulses, plus 2–3 hours

6 cups kala chana, picked over
1 cup vegetable oil
1 teaspoon chili powder
¼ teaspoon turmeric
1 teaspoon caraway seeds
1 teaspoon salt
6 garlic cloves, peeled and chopped
1 tablespoon tamarind paste (see note)
4 green chiles, seeded (optional)
1 tablespoon chopped parsley

Soak the kala chana overnight in plenty of cold water. Drain the pulses well.

Heat the oil in a saucepan over medium heat. When hot, add the chili powder, turmeric, and caraway seeds and cook 2–3 minutes.

Add the drained pulses, stir, and cook for 3–5 minutes more, stirring occasionally.

Add the salt, garlic, and the tamarind paste mixed in ½ cup water. Then add hot water and the chiles. Cover tightly and cook over low heat for 2–3 hours, until the pulses are tender, adding more water if necessary. Sprinkle with parsley before serving.

Note: Tamarind paste is the dark brown pulp of tamarind fruit that has been dried, then soaked and sieved. It has a sour fruity taste and is sold in many Indian food shops.

Green Dal with Tomato

Moong Dal

Preparation and cooking time: *Serves 8–10*
2 hours soaking, plus about 2¼ hours

1½ pounds hari dal, picked over
 ¼ cup vegetable oil
  1 medium-size onion, peeled and chopped
  1 teaspoon cumin seeds
  2 bay leaves, crumbled
 12 cherry tomatoes, or 6 small tomatoes
1¾ cups chicken stock
  1 teaspoon salt
  2 dried red chiles, seeded (optional) and chopped

Soak the beans in plenty of water for 2 hours. Drain them well.

Heat the oil in a saucepan over medium-low heat. When hot, add the onion, cumin, and bay leaves and cook, stirring occasionally, until the onion begins to brown.

Add the drained lentils, tomatoes, stock, salt, chiles, and 1 cup hot water. Bring the mixture to a boil, then simmer over low heat for 2 hours, until the pulses are tender, adding more water as necessary.

Oxtail Dal

Gayki Dum ki Dal

This is a delicious, spicy-hot dish I really like.

Preparation and cooking time: about 3 hours   *Serves 6–8*

4–6 tablespoons vegetable oil
  2 medium-size onions, peeled and chopped
  6 bay leaves, crumbled
 12 peppercorns
  2 cinnamon sticks, broken up
  2 pounds oxtail, cut in sections
  1 inch piece of fresh ginger root, chopped
  1 green chile, seeded (optional) and chopped
  1 teaspoon chili powder
  1 pound masoor dal, picked over, washed, and
    drained

Heat the oil in a large saucepan over medium-low heat. When hot, add the onions, bay leaves, peppercorns, and cinnamon sticks and cook for 5 minutes.

Turn the heat to medium-high, add the oxtail sections, and cook, stirring constantly, until they lose their raw color on all sides.

Add 6¼ cups water, the ginger, chile, and chili powder, bring to the boil, then cook over medium-low heat for 2 hours.

Add the drained pulses and 1 cup hot water. Cook over medium heat for 40 minutes, until the pulses and meat are tender. Serve with plain boiled rice.

Whole Green Lentils with Meat
Masoor ka Datcha

Some dal dishes are better very "wet," but I like this one on the dry side.

Preparation and cooking time: about 1½ hours   *Serves 6–8*

  1 cup vegetable oil
  1 large onion, peeled and chopped
  2 cinnamon sticks, broken up
  1 tablespoon caraway seeds
1¼ pounds continental masoor, picked over, washed, and drained well
  4 fresh green chiles, seeded (optional)
  8 cherry tomatoes, or 4 small tomatoes
  ½ inch piece of fresh ginger root, chopped
  1 pound lean beef or lamb with some bone, cut in small pieces

Heat the oil in a large saucepan over medium-low heat. When hot, add the onion, cinnamon, and caraway seeds and cook, stirring occasionally, until the onion begins to brown.

Add the lentils and let them cook 7–10 minutes, stirring occasionally.

Add the chiles, tomatoes, and ginger and cook for 7 more minutes, stirring occasionally.

Add 7 cups hot water, then the meat and bone.

Cook over low heat for another 45 minutes, stirring occasionally. The lentils should be tender and moist, not wet but not too dry. Serve with plain boiled rice and Cucumber Raita (page 140).

Spicy Chick-Peas

Chana Masaledar

If you are short of time, try this recipe using canned, drained chick-peas and about 1¼ cups water.

Preparation and cooking time: *Serves 4–6*
soaking the dried chick-peas, plus 3½–4½ hours

1¾ pounds kabli chana, picked over
6 tablespoons vegetable oil
4–6 bay leaves, crumbled
1 tablespoon cumin seeds
1¾ cups canned tomatoes
2 green chiles, seeded (optional)
2 teaspoons salt
2 garlic cloves, peeled and finely sliced
¼ cup chopped fresh parsley

Soak the chick-peas in plenty of cold water for 12 hours. Drain them well.

Heat 4 tablespoons of the oil in a saucepan over medium heat. Add the bay leaves and cumin and cook, stirring, for 1–2 minutes.

Add the canned tomatoes and their liquid, then add the chick-peas, chiles, salt, and 3¾ cups hot water.

Bring the liquid to the boil, reduce the heat, cover, and simmer for 3–4 hours, until the pulses are tender.

When the chick-peas are ready, heat the remaining 2 tablespoons oil in a small pan over medium-low heat. When hot, add the garlic and cook until the slices begin to brown, stirring occasionally.

Stir the garlic and the parsley into the chick-peas and cook for 10 minutes longer and serve.

12
Sweets

*I*ndian sweets are unlike any others in the world. Quantities of milk, nuts, raisins, and sugar are the basic ingredients. The display of sweets is an art in itself, and the *Halwais* (sweetmeat sellers) take great pride in presenting their specialities with care and finesse. The famous *Halwais* had their names stamped on their boxes, like chocolates in the West. Ghaseeta Ram in Bombay is particularly famous for rasmalai. In Delhi, Ghante Wala is known for his sohan halvah, which is brittle and made in the shape of a heart, with almonds and pistachios decorating it. I cannot give you this recipe as it is jealously guarded as a specialty, so instead I substitute a family version of a famous sweet recipe called sheer khorma.

Decorations of silver and gold foil pounded into feather-light sheets are often stuck on Indian sweets. Saffron is used in them a great deal, but it is now becoming prohibitive to use saffron in great quantities as it is so expensive. At weddings, receptions, and celebrations, great masses of sweets are consumed, and it is considered particularly auspicious to partake generously. Sweets are also the centerpiece of many religious festivals—sweets are brought to the homes of relatives and friends, and they in turn bring them to you.

One of the pleasures of living in a tropical place is the variety of fruits available, such as papaya, mango, custard apple, passionfruit, chikoo, ramphal, guava, six to eight different kinds of bananas, loquat, lichee, pineapple, sweet lime—all this in addition to more common fruits like apples, oranges, tangerines, watermelon, plums, peaches, apricots, cherries, etc. Growing up in Bombay, I have known all kinds of fruits and watched foreigners gingerly trying out local fruits for the first time. They often make a face.

There are ten to twelve different kinds of melons in India, but the best ones traditionally come from Afghanistan. Melons from Kabul almost have the consistency of an apple and are a cross in taste between a honeydew and a Cranshaw melon. Of course, we didn't have Cranshaw or honeydew melons in India; they were my introduction to melons in America. I also love the Charentelle melon from France, usually served with a squeeze of lemon or lime, Cointreau, and fresh mint. The mint is my added touch to this French dessert, as perfect with the melon as it is in complementing the spiciest Indian dishes.

The display of fruits closest to the ones I saw in the bazaars of my youth were those I saw in Paris while we were making Quartet. I made a sort of cornucopia of fruit salad for the cast and crew, adding mint, red wine, lemon juice, and cinnamon to the fruit, and let people top it off with thick crème fraîche if they wished. This feast of fruit helped me relive childhood experiences of shopping in the bazaars of Bombay.

Frozen Guava Cream
Sareefe ki Rabri

This is not really an ice cream, and if you, unlike me, have more time, you can chill the gelatin and the pudding in the refrigerator instead of the freezer.

Preparation and cooking time: *Serves 4–6*
25 minutes, plus 1–2 hours chilling

  2 large guavas
  ½ cup cold milk
1½ teaspoons powdered gelatin
1½ cups cold heavy cream
    Few drops of vanilla extract
    Confectioners' sugar, sifted

Spoon the pulp from the guavas, discarding the seeds and skin.

Heat half the milk over very low heat, stirring with a wooden spoon. When warmed, immediately pour the milk into a small bowl.

Sprinkle the gelatin into the hot milk and stir it briskly until it is dissolved. Put the mixture in the freezer until it begins to set.

Meanwhile, combine the rest of the milk with 1 cup of the cream in a bowl and whisk until thick. Add vanilla extract and sift in confectioners' sugar to taste.

Stir the guava pulp and thickened milk into the cream and pour the mixture into a serving bowl. Place in the freezer for 1–2 hours.

Whisk the remaining ½ cup cream until thick and decorate the pudding with it.

Carrot Halva

Gajjar ka Halva

Preparation and cooking time: 1 hour   *Serves 6*

Pinch of saffron
½ cup heavy cream
¼ pound butter
1½ pounds carrots, peeled and grated
¼ cup sugar
4 tablespoons raisins
Seeds from 4 black cardamoms
20 blanched almonds, sliced lengthwise into slivers
1 tablespoon rose water
Heavy cream, to serve (optional)

Gently stir the saffron into 2 tablespoons of the cream and gradually mix in the rest of the cream. It will take on the color of the saffron. Do not beat the mixture.

Melt the butter in a heavy saucepan over low heat. Add the grated carrots and stir to coat well.

Stir the sugar, raisins, and cardamom seeds into the carrot mixture.

Blend in the saffron and cream mixture, then the almonds. Sprinkle in the rose water and cook for 30–40 minutes over a low heat, stirring occasionally. The mixture will become a fairly dry, golden-brown mass.

Serve the halva with heavy cream poured over the top, if wished.

Quartet Fruit Salad
Quartet *Phal ka Salaad*

This is a dessert served in the film *Quartet*.

Preparation time: *Serves 8–10*
15 minutes, plus chilling

1¾ cups good red Beaujolais wine
  4 teaspoons sugar
  2 cinnamon sticks, broken in pieces
    Juice of 4 lemons
  2 pints ripe strawberries, hulled
  4 kiwi fruit, peeled and sliced
  2 apples, cored and cubed
  1 pound cherries, pitted
1½ pounds ripe peaches, peeled, seeded, and sliced
  4 sprigs of fresh mint, stems removed

Pour the wine into a large bowl and add the sugar, cinnamon, and lemon juice. Prepare the rest of the ingredients in the order listed, stirring them immediately into the wine mixture.

Chill the mixture in the refrigerator at least 2 hours before serving.

Note: Though this salad is perfect on its own, you can gild the lily by serving it with crème fraîche.

Stewed Spiced Pears
Naaspati ka Murabba

Preparation and cooking time: 50 minutes   *Serves 6*

1½ lemons
 12 firm, ripe pears, peeled, cored, and cut into slices
  1 cup sugar
  1 teaspoon vanilla essence
  3 cinnamon sticks
 ½ teaspoon ground cinnamon
  3 ounces whole, blanched almonds
    Heavy cream, to serve (optional)

Put the lemons in a food processor fitted with the steel blade and process until the lemons are a coarse paste.

Put the lemon paste in a large saucepan with the pears, sugar, vanilla, cinnamon sticks, ground cinnamon, and almonds. Cover and cook over medium-low heat for 40 minutes, stirring occasionally.

Remove the cinnamon sticks and serve the stewed pears with heavy cream, if wished.

Cinnamon-Brandy Baked Pears
Darchini-Walli Dum Naaspati

Preparation and cooking time: about 30 minutes   *Serves 6–8*

9 medium-ripe pears
⅓ cup brandy
½ teaspoon vanilla essence
1 teaspoon ground cinnamon
2 tablespoons sugar
   Whipped cream, to serve

Heat the oven to 375°F. Meanwhile, halve the pears and remove the cores carefully with a spoon or paring knife. Place the pears in a baking dish.

Combine the brandy and vanilla and pour this over the pears.

Sprinkle the cinnamon and sugar over the mixture and bake, covered, for 15–20 minutes. The pears should be tender but not too soft.

Serve the pears warm, with whipped cream served separately.

Orange Wheels

Santre ke Chakle

Preparation time: 10 minutes, plus chilling   *Serves 4–6*

- 6 large oranges
- ¼ cup sugar
- 2 tablespoons raisins
- 1 teaspoon ground nutmeg or cinnamon
- 4 tablespoons rose water
  Juice of ½ lemon
- 2 tablespoons Grand Marnier or other orange liqueur

Peel the oranges, carefully removing all the yellow pith. Slice each one across into 4–5 rounds and put them into a large shallow bowl.

Combine the sugar, raisins, nutmeg or cinnamon, rose water, lemon juice, and Grand Marnier, pour the mixture over the orange wheels and refrigerate them for at least 2 hours.

Serve the orange wheels, chilled, with some of their juice.

Watermelon Ice Delight
Tarbooj ki Kheer

Preparation time: 30 minutes, plus freezing   *Serves 4–6*

- 1 small watermelon
- 1½ tablespoons gelatin
- 2 tablespoons milk
- ½ cup plus 2 tablespoons cream
  Few drops of vanilla essence
  Confectioners' sugar
- 2 medium-size egg whites

Halve the melon and scoop out most of the flesh. Remove the seeds and process the flesh into a slush in a food processor or blender.

Soak the gelatin in ½ cup water and heat the mixture over low heat until the gelatin dissolves.

Cool the gelatin mixture slightly and add it to the watermelon.

Combine the milk and the cream and whisk until the cream is thick. Flavor the cream with vanilla essence and a little confectioners' sugar to taste. Stir the cream into the watermelon.

Beat the egg whites until they are stiff but not dry. Fold them well into the melon mixture.

Pour the mixture into a decorative metal mould and freeze for at least 4 hours.

Dip the mold in hot water and turn the desert out onto a serving plate. Serve immediately.

Spiced Fresh Pineapple
Masaledar Ananas

Preparation time: Serves 4–6
chilling the pineapple, plus 10 minutes

1 chilled pineapple
   Ground cinnamon or freshly grated nutmeg

Peel and slice the pineapple. Place the slices on a serving dish
and sprinkle cinnamon or nutmeg over them.
   Note: A little vanilla essence is another delightful addition to
sprinkle over this simple, superb dessert.

Pistachio-Almond Milk Pudding
Sheer Khorma

On feast days, Chicken Korma (page 83) was often served,
accompanied by a raita made from cucumber, onions, and
tomatoes mixed in lots of yoghurt. A special bread made in the
Muslim areas of Bombay always accompanied these dishes. It
was made of layer upon layer of very thin dough topped with
nuts. Such a meal would especially be served on Id, the day
after the Muslim month of fasting, Ramzan. But the first thing
that one ate in the morning after prayers was something sweet.
For this special treat, Mother would get up at four in the
morning and prepare sheer khorma. Fresh milk was brought
(it seemed like gallons), and she would cook it slowly and
gently in a huge pot.
   Meanwhile, we bathed and got ready to go to the mosque
for prayers. We were always dressed in completely new

clothes, everything new for Id. I remember the crisp smell of these new clothes: kurtas, pyjamas, caps, everything. After prayers we came home to eat the sweet sheer khorma and then were taken to visit family and friends where we children would collect gifts of money. After a month of fasting, everyone so enjoyed Id, which is a bit like Easter in Christian countries.

On these visits, we were always offered, on a silver tray, or *thali,* a perfumed essence called *ittar,* the fragrance of which came from the finest natural extracts, rose, mogra, chameli, hina. It was applied, by stopper, to the right hand and ear lobes. Sometimes it spilled onto our clothing and the fragrance seemed to last forever. These rituals meant so much as they bound us together, family and friends.

Preparation and cooking time: *Serves 12*
overnight soaking, plus about 40 minutes

- ¾ **pound shelled unsalted pistachios**
- 3 **ounces shelled, unskinned almonds**
- 2 **ounces dried vermicelli**
- ¼ **pound butter**
- 5 **cups milk**
- ¾ **cup cream**
- ½ **teaspoon saffron**
- 5 **tablespoons sugar**

Place the pistachios and almonds in a bowl and add cold water to cover. Let them stand overnight, then drain and rub off the skins with a tea cloth.

Coarsely grind the nuts in a food processor or blender. Do not grind them to a paste.

Break the vermicelli in pieces about 4 inches long. Melt the butter in a large saucepan and add the vermicelli. Cook, stirring, until the vermicelli is nicely browned without burning.

Add the milk and cream and bring to the boil.

Reduce the heat, add the pistachio mixture, saffron, and sugar and simmer, stirring often, about 15 minutes. Spoon into bowls and serve hot.

Sweet Saffron Rice with Nuts
Meethi Taheeri

Preparation and cooking time: *Serves 4*
cooking the rice, plus 12–15 minutes

2 cups sugar
¼ teaspoon powdered saffron
3 tablespoons butter
8 cloves
1 cup cooked long-grain rice (¼ cup uncooked rice)
2 tablespoons slivered almonds
¼ cup seedless raisins

Simmer the sugar and ½ cup water until thick and syrupy, 2–3 minutes. Stir in the saffron.

Melt the butter in another saucepan over medium-low heat, add the cloves, and cook until the cloves begin to sputter.

Add the rice and sugar syrup, stir well, and add the nuts and raisins. Simmer the mixture, covered, for 5 minutes. Serve hot.

Festive Sweet Yoghurt
Shrikund

Preparation time: *Serves 4–6*
2–3 hours draining, plus 10 minutes, then chilling

4 cups plain yoghurt
1 ounce shelled almonds
1 ounce shelled, unsalted pistachios
½ cup confectioners' sugar
½ teaspoon ground cardamom
¼ teaspoon saffron powder
2 tablespoons rose water

Pour the yoghurt into the middle of a large piece of cheese-cloth, gather the corners together and tie them with string. Hang the cheesecloth over a bowl for 2–3 hours to drain off the excess water.

Meanwhile, drop the nuts in boiling water and cook for 1 minute. Drain them well and rub off the skins with a tea cloth.

Turn the yoghurt into a clean bowl, add the sugar, and mix the two together thoroughly.

Stir in the cardamom, saffron, and rose water. Pour the mixture into a glass serving bowl and sprinkle the nuts over the top. Chill well to serve.

Indian Rice Pudding
Kheer

Preparation and cooking time: 1 hour, plus cooling   *Serves 6–8*

½ cup long-grain rice
5¾ cups milk
1 cup sugar
¼ cup dried milk
1 tablespoon rose water
6–8 blanched almonds, chopped
10–12 shelled, unsalted pistachios, chopped
¼ cup seedless raisins

Boil the rice in 3¼ cups water until the rice is very soft.

Heat the milk and sugar in another pan and bring them to the boil.

Immediately reduce the heat and stir in the softened rice. Continue cooking over medium-low heat, stirring, until the mixture becomes thick.

Add the dried milk and stir in well.

Add the rose water, almonds, pistachios, and raisins and remove from the heat.

Let the pudding cool and serve it at room temperature.

Rice, Pistachio, and Almond Pudding

Feerni

Preparation and cooking time:　　　　　*Serves 4–6*
about 25 minutes, plus chilling

- 6½ cups milk
- 1 cup sugar
- ¼ cup cracked rice
- ¼ cup dried milk
- 6–8 shelled, blanched almonds
- 10 shelled, unsalted pistachios
- Pinch of ground cardamom

Mix the milk and sugar, adding more sugar, if wished, and heat in a heavy saucepan over medium-high heat.

Stir the cracked rice into 1 cup water.

When the milk begins to boil, remove the pan from the heat and vigorously whisk in the rice liquid to avoid lumps.

When the mixture is smooth, place it over medium-low heat, stir in the dried milk, and cook until thick, whisking occasionally.

Stir in the nuts and cardamom, pour the mixture into small serving bowls, and cool. Serve at room temperature or lightly chilled.

Almond Sweetmeat

Badam Paparh

Preparation time: *Serves 6–8*
20–25 minutes, plus 6–8 hours drying

1¼ cups blanched almonds
 ½ cup soft brown sugar

Pound and grind the almonds in a mortar until they become
an oily mass. Alternatively, grind the almonds in a food processor or chop, then grind them in batches in a blender until
oily.

Add the sugar and knead the mixture well until it is very
smooth and soft.

Divide the almond mixture into 4–6 portions and roll each
into a ball. Lightly coat the balls with superfine sugar and roll
each one out into a thin round.

Leave the portions to dry on cheesecloth for 6–8 hours.

Store separately in greaseproof paper in an airtight container for up to 2 weeks.

13

Pickles and Chutneys

I first began to cook in earnest in 1958, when I was on my own in New York. Up to then I had dabbled from time to time with cooking, at Boy Scout outings or school picnics. But in India cooking in the home is not really something family men do. Cooking is either done by a hired cook (often a man) or, more usually, by one's mother and sisters. As a child I spent a certain amount of time in the kitchen, the center of activity in our large household. I watched and listened and tasted continually. Shopping with my father and hearing the family's many discussions and comments about food, I quite naturally absorbed a great deal without being aware. These things awakened my interest in cooking and made it quite a natural part of life.

It dawned on me that each family has a distinctive way of cooking, passed on from one generation to the next. This is why the same classic Indian dishes never taste exactly the same in different homes you visit. Each one has its own style or "taste" somehow bequeathed by grandmother to mother to daughters and, occasionally, to a son like myself. If my father were ever to cook, I'm sure he would also make wonderful dishes with the same family "taste."

In this chapter I have included some of my family's recipes for pickles. You will also find a recipe for Hamida Begum's Lime Pickle, which figures so importantly in my film *The Courtesans of Bombay*. It is a very old recipe and is one of the few in this book that will really take a lot of time to make. But the result is well worth the effort.

In India we never stored pickles and chutneys in the refrigerator, but in a cool, dark area. Because I always have a refrigerator available, I tend to store my pickles and chutneys, well sealed, in it.

Tomato Chutney
Tamatar Chutni

Preparation and cooking time:
2¼–2¾ hours, plus cooling

Makes about 2 pints

- 2 lemons
- 5 pounds tomatoes
- 1¼ cups white wine vinegar
- 1½ cups sugar
- 2 teaspoons cayenne pepper
- 5 ounces raisins
- 1 cinnamon stick, broken into small pieces
- 5 ounces slivered almonds

Seed and chop the lemons, reserving the juice. Transfer the lemons and juice to a food processor or in batches to a blender and process them to shreds.

Combine the tomatoes, vinegar, sugar, cayenne pepper, raisins, cinnamon, almonds, shredded lemons, and 1¾ cups water in a deep saucepan. Bring the mixture to a boil.

Reduce the heat and simmer, stirring occasionally, until the liquid boils almost all away, 2–2½ hours.

Remove the chutney from the heat and let it cool. Transfer it to a clean glass or ceramic jar or jars and cover with a nonmetallic, airtight lid or lids. Store in a cool, dark place or the refrigerator.

Mixed Vegetable Pickle

Sabzi ka Aachar

Preparation and cooking time: *Makes about 2 pints*
1 hour soaking, plus 30 minutes, then cooling

  1 medium-size cauliflower
  ¼ pound green beans, topped and tailed and cut across in half
  1 medium-size carrot
1¼ cups distilled or white wine vinegar
  ¾ cup vegetable oil
  8 bay leaves, crumbled
12 garlic cloves, peeled and roughly chopped
  2 tablespoons sugar
  6 black peppercorns
    Salt

For the masala
  9 red chiles, seeded (optional) and chopped
  ½ teaspoon yellow mustard seeds
  ½ teaspoon ground fenugreek leaves
  2 inch piece of fresh ginger root, grated
  3 green chiles, seeded (optional)
  2 teaspoons cumin seeds

Cut the cauliflower into florets and the carrot into slices about ¼ inch thick.

Mix and wash the vegetables, then cover them with fresh cold water for 1 hour.

Drain the vegetables well and leave them in a colander.

Grind the masala spices together in a mortar, adding a little of the vinegar to make a paste.

Heat the oil in a large frying pan over medium-low heat. When hot, add the bay leaves and garlic and cook, stirring frequently, for 2–3 minutes.

Add the masala paste to the pan and fry for 5 minutes longer.

Add the sugar, vegetables, peppercorns, salt to taste, and remaining vinegar to the pan. Cook over low heat until the vegetables soften.

Remove the mixture from the heat and let it cool. Transfer it to a clean glass or ceramic jar and cover with a nonmetallic, airtight lid. Store in a cool, dark place or the refrigerator.

Broccoli Pickle

Broccoli ka Aachar

Preparation time: *Makes about 2 pints*
15 minutes, plus 1 week maturing

- 3 pounds broccoli, cut into florets with tender stems attached
- 1 bunch of dill, stemmed and chopped
- 1 tablespoon yellow mustard seeds
- 5–10 garlic cloves, peeled and chopped
- 1¼ cups vinegar
- 1 teaspoon salt
- 1 tablespoon vegetable oil
- 1 inch piece of fresh ginger root, coarsely grated

Put all the ingredients and 1¼ cups water into a glass jar or jars and top with nonmetallic, airtight lids. Shake to mix well.

Allow the pickle to mature in a cool, dark place for 1 week, shaking occasionally.

Parveen's Tomato Chutney
Parveen ki Tamatar Chutni

Preparation and cooking time: Makes about 1¾ cups
3–3½ hours

- 3½ pounds tomatoes
- 1¾ cups white wine vinegar
- ½ teaspoon salt
- 2 tablespoons raisins
- 2 inch piece of fresh ginger root, finely grated
- 1 garlic clove, peeled and pressed
- 1½ teaspoons ground cumin
- ½ teaspoon cumin seeds
- 8 cloves
- 6–8 black peppercorns
- 1 cinnamon stick, broken in pieces
- ½ cup sugar
- 2 teaspoons chili powder

Wash the tomatoes, shake them dry, and put them in a large saucepan with 1½ cups of the vinegar and salt. Cover and heat them until the vinegar boils, then reduce the heat and simmer, uncovered, until the tomatoes become just tender, 8–10 minutes.

Remove the tomatoes from the pan with a slotted spoon and set them aside.

Meanwhile, soak the raisins in the remaining ¼ cup vinegar for at least 30 minutes.

Mix the ginger, garlic, and ground cumin to a fine paste. Mix in the cumin seeds and reserve.

Pound the cloves, peppercorns, and cinnamon together in a mortar.

Put the tomatoes in a dry saucepan, add the sugar, and place over medium-low heat. Cook until the sugar melts, stirring occasionally.

Add the garlic paste and the clove mixture to the pan, then stir in the raisins and their soaking liquid and the chili powder. Cover and cook for 2 hours, until the mixture is thick.

Remove the pan from the heat, add salt if necessary, and allow the chutney to cool completely.

Transfer the chutney to clean glass or ceramic jars and cover with nonmetallic, airtight lids. Store in a cool, dark place or the refrigerator.

Green Chile and Lime Pickle
Hari Mirch Nimboo ka Aachar

Preparation and cooking time: 30 minutes, plus cooling

Makes about 2 pints

- 1 pound green chiles
- 15 limes
- 3 tablespoons dry mustard
- ½ cup salt
- 1 cup vegetable oil
- ½ teaspoon ground asafetida
- ¼ teaspoon ground fenugreek leaves
- 1 teaspoon turmeric

Wash the chiles, removing any stalks, and dry them well.

Cut the limes in half, extract the juice, and discard the flesh.

Mix the lime juice with the mustard and salt.

Heat the oil until nearly boiling. Remove it from the heat and add the asafetida, fenugreek, and turmeric.

Stir in the mustard mixture and green chiles, mixing well. When cool, transfer the mixture to clean glass or ceramic jars and cover with nonmetallic, airtight lids. Store in a cool, dark place or the refrigerator.

Spicy Carrot Hors d'Oeuvre

Gajjar ka Aachar

Preparation time: *Serves 4*
5–10 minutes, plus chilling

- 6 medium-size carrots
- ¼ cup vegetable oil
- 1–1½ teaspoons chili powder
- 1 tablespoon caraway seeds
- Juice of ½ lemon
- ½ teaspoon salt
- 2 teaspoons chopped fresh dill, or ½ teaspoon dill weed (optional)

Cut the carrots lengthwise into sticks, then halve them once and place them in a bowl.

Whisk the oil, chili powder, caraway seeds, lemon juice, and salt together.

Pour the mixture over the carrot sticks, toss well, and refrigerate. Serve chilled, sprinkled, if wished, with chopped fresh dill or dill weed. Keeps refrigerated, covered, up to a week.

Mango Chutney
Ambia ki Chutni

Preparation and cooking time: *Makes about 1¾ cups*
about 40 minutes, plus overnight maceration and cooling

2¼ pounds ripe mangoes
1¾ cups vinegar
3¼ cups soft dark brown sugar
     Salt
1½ teaspoons chili powder
  1 inch piece of fresh ginger root, finely chopped
  ½ cup assorted chopped dried fruit and nuts such as
     raisins, currants, walnuts, dates, and cashews

Peel the mangoes, then cut the flesh into slices.

Place the raw mangoes in a glass or ceramic bowl or other container and add the vinegar, soft dark brown sugar, salt, chili powder, and chopped ginger. Stir well, cover, and leave overnight to macerate.

The next day, transfer the mixture to a stainless steel saucepan and cook over low heat, stirring frequently, until the mixture begins to thicken.

Add the chopped fruit and nuts and continue cooking, stirring frequently to prevent burning, until the mixture is thick.

Remove the pan from the heat. When the chutney is cool enough, correct the seasoning with more salt, chili powder, and vinegar to taste.

Transfer the chutney to a clean dry glass or ceramic jar or jars and seal with nonmetalic, airtight lids. Store in a cool, dark place or the refrigerator.

Hamida Begum's Stuffed Lime Pickle

Bhare Nimboo ka Aachar

This recipe, which figures prominently in *The Courtesans of Bombay,* will produce enough pickle to last an entire family for quite a long time, as one can imagine. It is so good that there is always great demand for it from friends and family. You can, of course, reduce the quantities proportionally.

Preparation and cooking time: *Makes about 10 pints*
2½–3 hours, plus cooling and bottling

- **200 limes**
- **1¼ pounds dried red chiles**
- **1 cup mustard seeds**
- **½ cup cumin seeds**
- **½ cup onion seeds**
- **1 pound garlic cloves, peeled**
- **1 pound salt**
- **3¾ cups mustard oil**
- **12 green chiles**

Squeeze the juice of 100 of the limes into a large bowl, cover, and reserve.

Put the rest of the limes in a large saucepan or preserving pan, cover with plenty of water, bring to a boil, and simmer until they are tender.

Drain the limes, dry them with a tea towel, and put them aside.

Pound the red chiles fine in a mortar or grind them in a food processor or in batches in a blender.

Put the mustard seeds in a frying pan over low heat and dry-roast them for 2–3 minutes, shaking the pan occasionally. The seeds should begin to release their aroma.

Repeat with the cumin seeds and then the onion seeds.

Combine the mustard, cumin, and onion seeds. Take two-thirds of the mixture and pound it fine in a mortar or grind it in a food processor or in batches in a blender.

Blend the remaining seed mixture with the ground red chiles and the pounded or ground seed mixture.

Pound the garlic cloves to a paste in a mortar or a food processor or in batches in a blender with a little water, then drain off the water.

Mix the garlic with the chile and seed mixture, adding the salt and a little of the lime juice to make a paste.

Cut the boiled limes halfway down into four. Spread the spice paste well into the limes, put them in a large container, and add the rest of the lime juice.

Warm the oil until it begins to sputter, then pour it over the stuffed limes and whole green chiles.

When the mixture is cool enough, transfer it to glass or ceramic bottles and cover with nonmetallic, airtight lids. Store in a cool, dark place or the refrigerator.

Coconut and Mint Chutney
Khopra Poodina Chutni

This is delicious with roasted meats and fowl.

Preparation and cooking time: 50 minutes–1 hour   *Serves 6–8*

1 **fresh coconut**
  Leaves of 4 mint sprigs
  Juice of 1 lemon
2 **hot green chiles, seeded (optional)**

Heat the oven to 400°F.

Bake the coconut for 15 minutes.

Place the hot coconut on concrete or another hard surface and smash it open with a hammer.

When the coconut pieces are cool enough, peel away the brown papery skin and the white meat with a potato peeler. Chop any large pieces, if necessary, into smaller ones.

Put the coconut and the rest of the ingredients in a food processor or blender, in batches and with a little extra water if necessary, and process the mixture to a paste. Serve the chutney fresh. It can be stored, well covered, in the refrigerator for 1–2 days.

Sweet Peach Chutney

Meethe Shaftaloo ki Chutni

This sweet chutney is great when used as a complement to main dishes or to top ice cream as a dessert

Preparation and cooking time: about 3 hours, plus cooling

Makes about 6 pints

- 10 pounds firm ripe peaches
- 2 cinnamon sticks
- 1 cup medium-dry sherry
- 6 cardamom pods
- 1 pound sugar
- 5 ounces raisins
- ½ cup lemon juice
- 1 teaspoon almond extract

Heat a large saucepan of water to the boil and remove from heat. Drop in 8–12 peaches, leave for 1 minute, then remove 1 peach and peel off the skin and set it aside. Repeat with the other peaches in the water.

Continue soaking the rest of the peaches, a few at a time, in the hot water, reheating it if necessary, peeling and setting them aside.

Halve and stone the peaches, then chop the flesh.

Combine the peaches, cinnamon, sherry, cardamom pods, sugar, raisins, lemon juice, and almond extract in a large saucepan or preserving pan. Bring the mixture to a boil, stirring frequently.

Reduce the heat and simmer over medium-low heat for 2 hours, stirring frequently, until the mixture becomes very thick. Reduce the heat, if necessary, to prevent burning.

When the chutney is cool enough, transfer it to clean, dry glass or ceramic jars and cover with nonmetallic, airtight lids. Store in a cool, dark place or the refrigerator.

Ginger Pickle

Adrak ka Aachar

Preparation time:　　　　　　　　　　*Makes about 1¾ cups*
10 minutes, plus 1 week maturing

  8　pieces fresh ginger root, each about 4 inches long,
     finely peeled
3¾　cups distilled or white wine vinegar
1¼　cups mustard oil
  2　tablespoons yellow mustard seeds
12　garlic cloves, peeled and halved lengthwise
  ½　tablespoon salt
  6　green chiles

Put all the ingredients in a large glass jar or jars and top with nonmetallic, airtight lids. Shake to mix well.

Allow the pickle to mature for 1 week in a cool, dark place, shaking occasionally.

Cauliflower Pickle
Phool Gobi ka Aachar

Preparation and cooking time: *Makes about 1¾ cups*
10 minutes, plus 1 week maturing

    1 medium-size cauliflower, cut into florets
    1 green chile, seeded (optional) and chopped
 5–10 garlic cloves, peeled and coarsely chopped
  1¼ cups vinegar
    2 teaspoons salt
    1 teaspoon turmeric
    1 teaspoon caraway seeds
    2 inch piece of fresh ginger root, coarsely grated
    1 tablespoon vegetable oil

Put all the ingredients and 1¼ cups water into a large glass jar or jars and top with nonmetallic, airtight lids. Shake to mix well.

Alllow the pickle to mature for 1 week in a cool, dark place, shaking occasionally.

Mango Relish
Aam Chhunda

Preparation and cooking time: about 40 minutes, plus cooling

Makes about 1¾ cups

2¼ pounds mangoes
2¼ pounds sugar
4 tablespoons salt
5–6 black peppercorns
1½ teaspoons chili powder
2–3 black cardamom pods, coarsely pounded

Wash, dry, peel, and grate the mangoes into a saucepan.

Stir in the sugar and place the pan over low heat, stirring occasionally with a wooden spoon, for about 30 minutes.

When the mixture changes color and falls in a thread when lifted with the spoon, remove from heat.

Stir in the salt, pepper, and chili powder with the coarsely pounded cardamom pods. Let the mixture cool.

Transfer the mixture to a clean, dry glass jar and cover with a nonmetallic, airtight lid. Store in a cool, dark place or the refrigerator.

INDEX